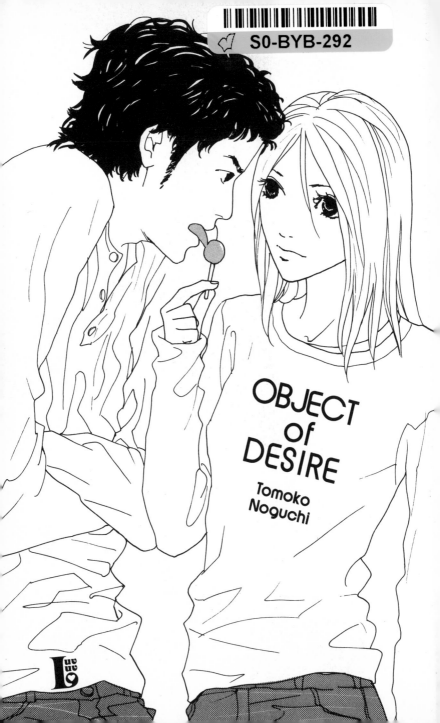

OBJECT
of
DESIRE

Tomoko
Noguchi

CONTENTS

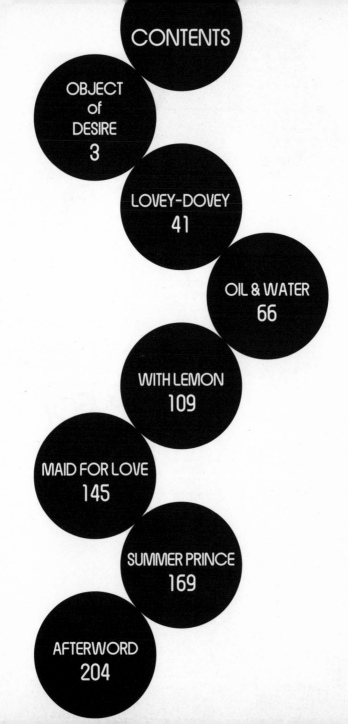

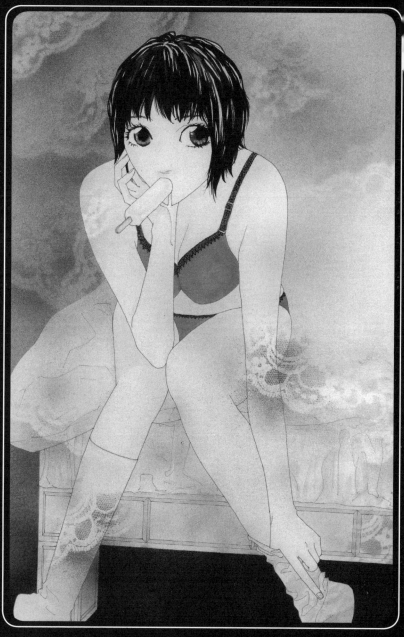

OBJECT OF DESIRE

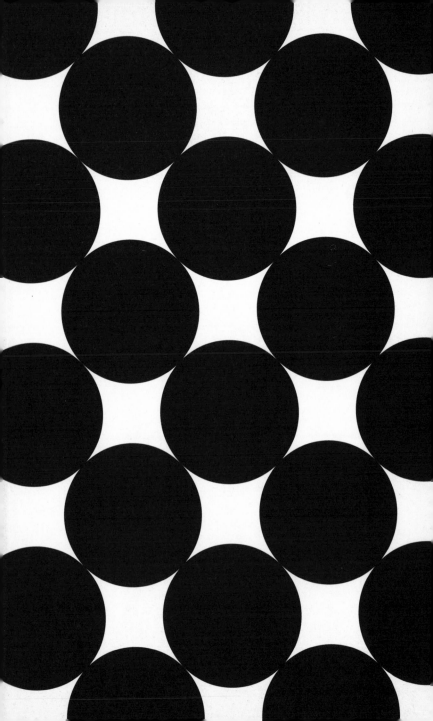

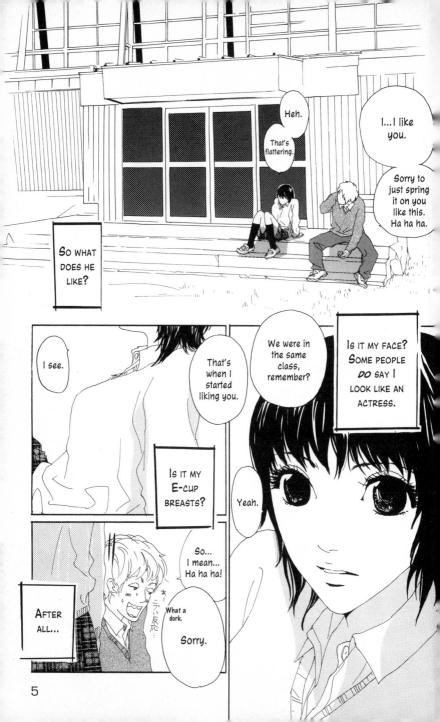

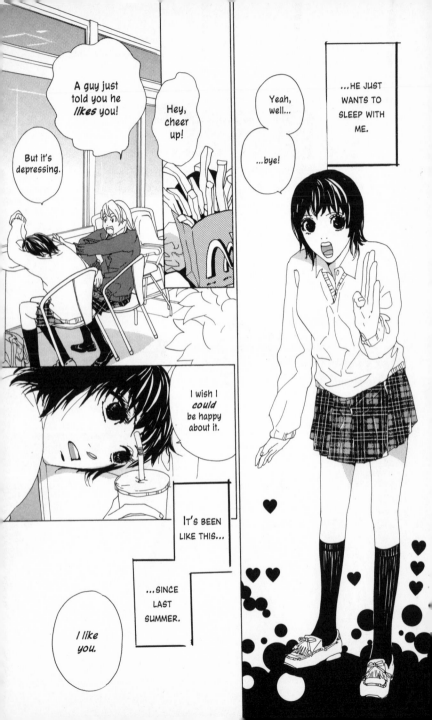

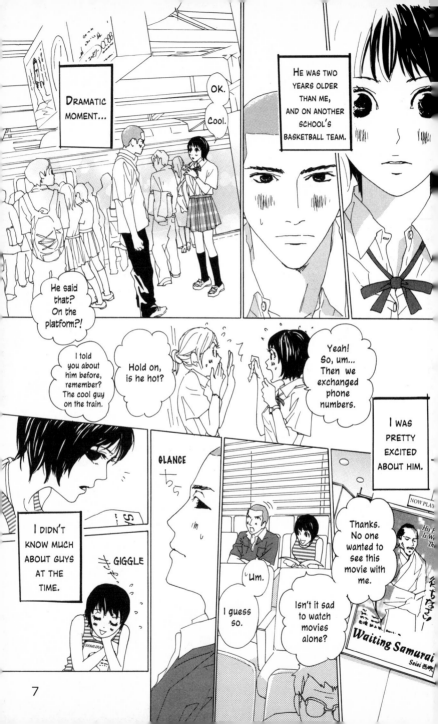

DRAMATIC MOMENT...

OK.

Cool.

HE WAS TWO YEARS OLDER THAN ME, AND ON ANOTHER SCHOOL'S BASKETBALL TEAM.

He said that? On the platform?!

I told you about him before, remember? The cool guy on the train.

Hold on, is he hot?

Yeah! So, um... Then we exchanged phone numbers.

I WAS PRETTY EXCITED ABOUT HIM.

GLANCE

NOW PLAY

I DIDN'T KNOW MUCH ABOUT GUYS AT THE TIME.

GIGGLE

Thanks. No one wanted to see this movie with me.

Um.

I guess so.

Isn't it sad to watch movies alone?

Waiting Samurai

Seiei

7

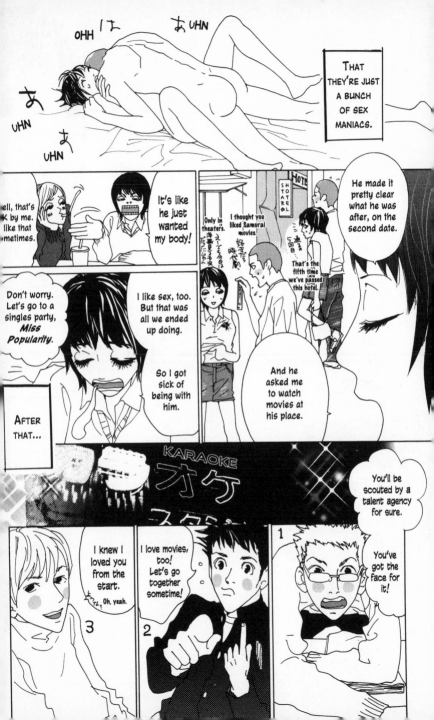

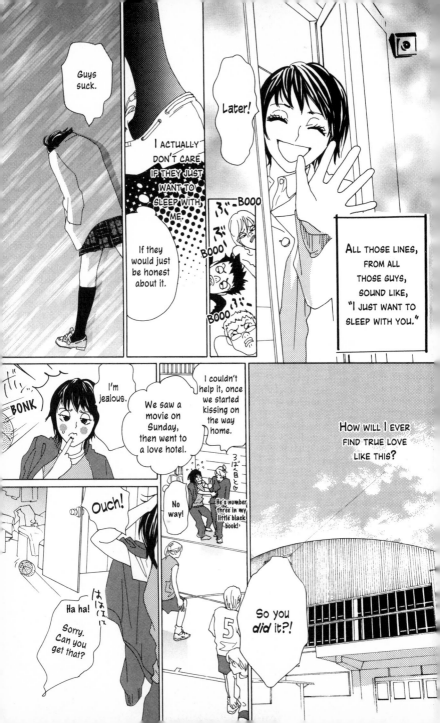

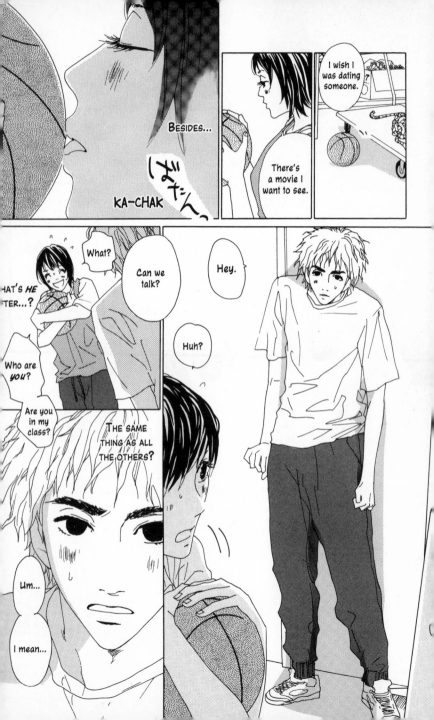

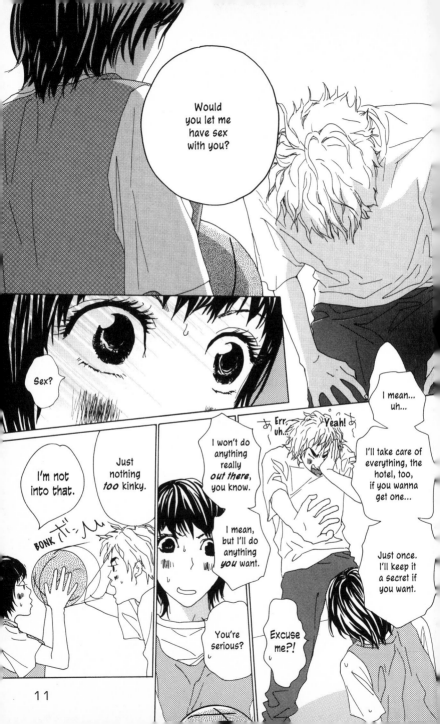

Would you let me have sex with you?

Sex?

I mean... uh...

Err. uh...

Yeah!

I'll take care of everything, the hotel, too, if you wanna get one...

I won't do anything really *out there*, you know.

Just nothing *too* kinky.

I'm not into that.

BONK

I mean, but I'll do anything *you* want.

Just once. I'll keep it a secret if you want.

You're serious?

Excuse me?!

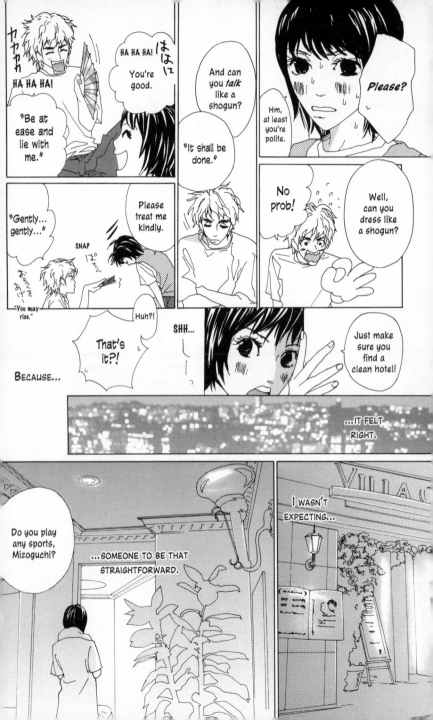

HA HA HA!

"Be at ease and lie with me."

HA HA HA!

You're good.

And can you *talk* like a shogun?

"It shall be done."

Please?

Hm, at least you're polite.

"Gently... gently..."

SNAP

"You may rise."

Please treat me kindly.

Huh?!

No prob!

Well, can you dress like a shogun?

That's it?!

SHH...

Just make sure you find a clean hotel!

BECAUSE...

...IT FELT RIGHT.

Do you play any sports, Mizoguchi?

...SOMEONE TO BE THAT STRAIGHTFORWARD.

I WASN'T EXPECTING...

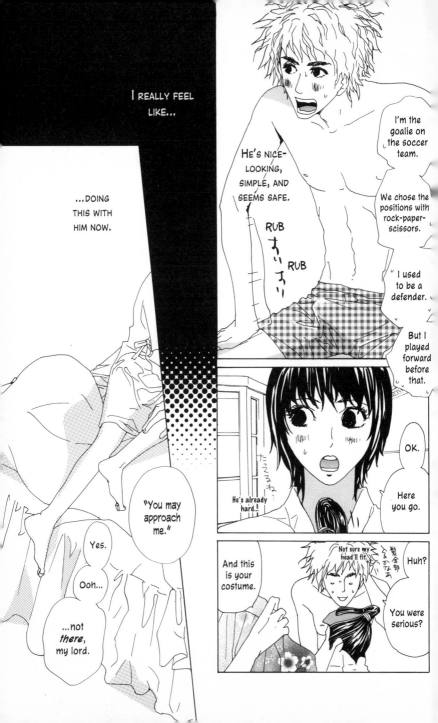

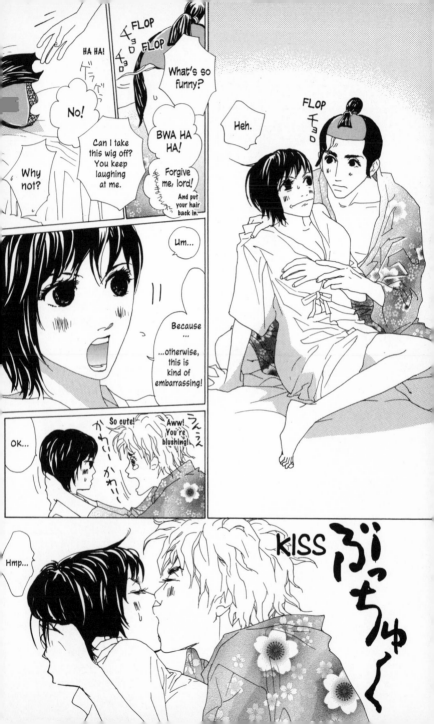

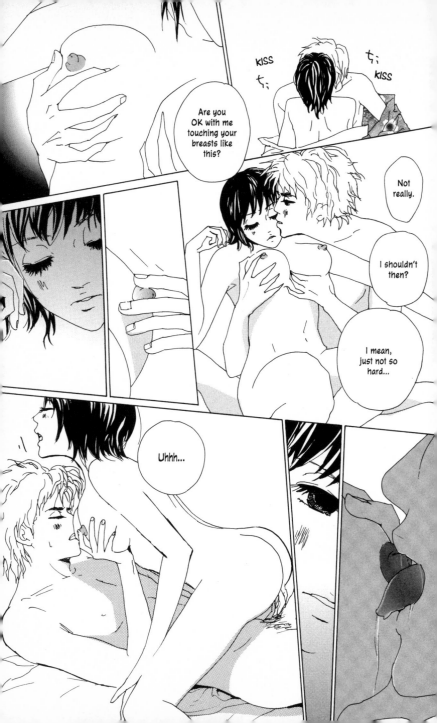

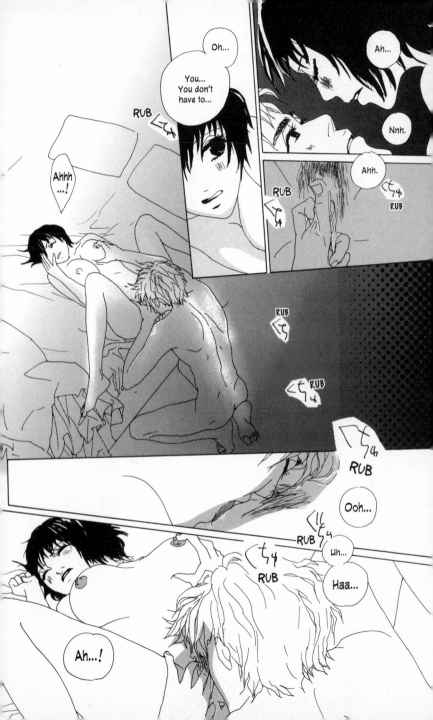

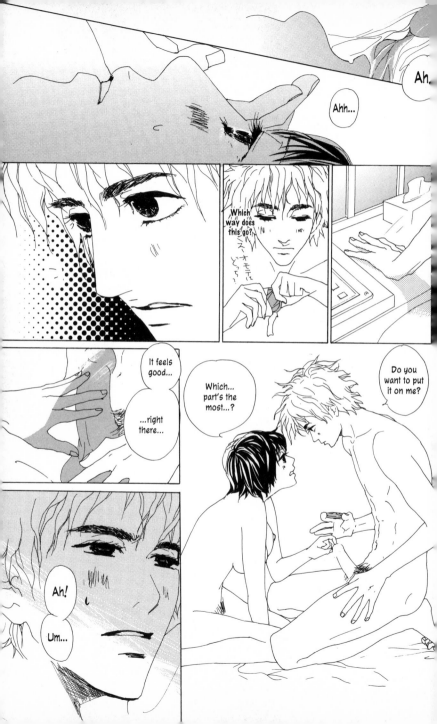

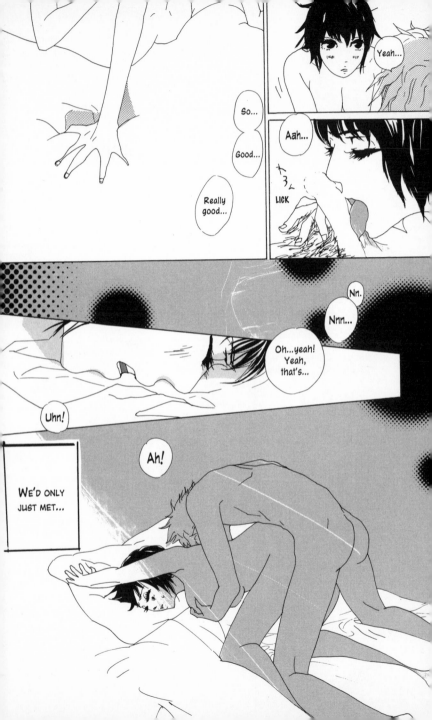

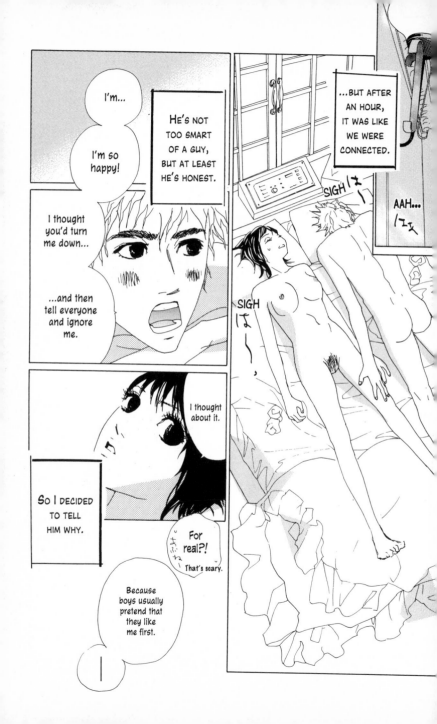

I'm...

I'm so happy!

HE'S NOT TOO SMART OF A GUY, BUT AT LEAST HE'S HONEST.

...BUT AFTER AN HOUR, IT WAS LIKE WE WERE CONNECTED.

I thought you'd turn me down...

...and then tell everyone and ignore me.

AAH...

SIGH

SIGH

I thought about it.

So I DECIDED TO TELL HIM WHY.

For real?!

That's scary.

Because boys usually pretend that they like me first.

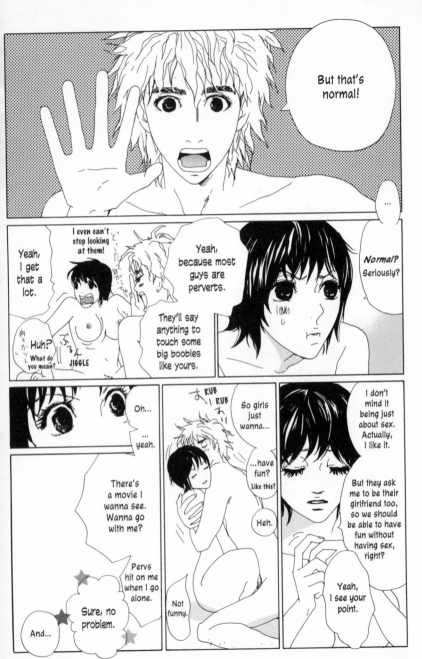

20

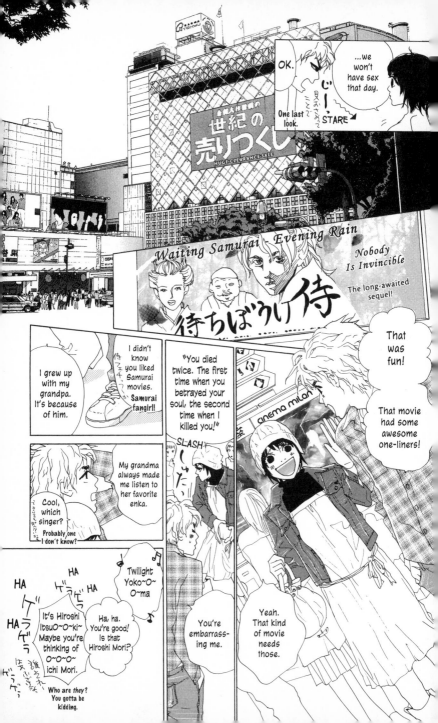

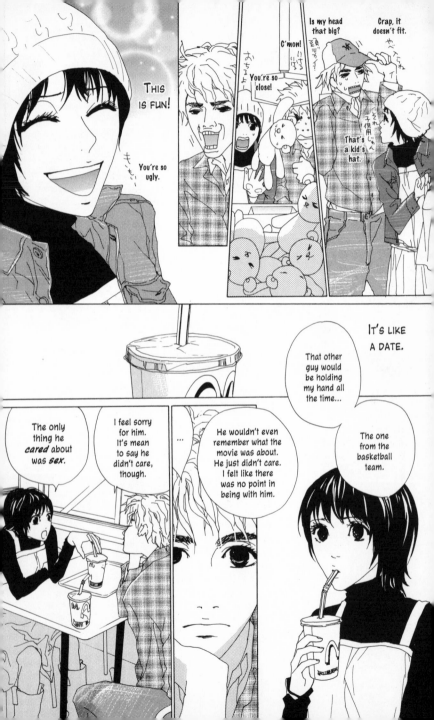

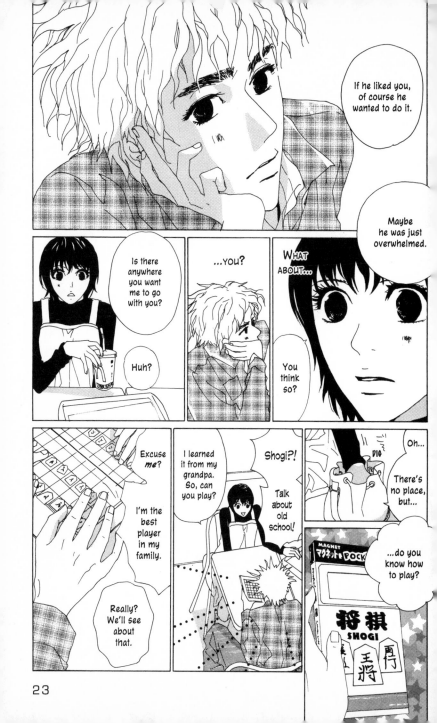

If he liked you, of course he wanted to do it.

Maybe he was just overwhelmed.

Is there anywhere you want me to go with you?

Huh?

...YOU?

WHAT ABOUT...

You think so?

Excuse *me*?

I'm the best player in my family.

Really? We'll see about that.

I learned it from my grandpa. So, can you play?

Shogi?!

Talk about old school!

DIG

Oh...

There's no place, but...

...do you know how to play?

MAGNET マグネット POCK

将棋 SHOGI

王将

23

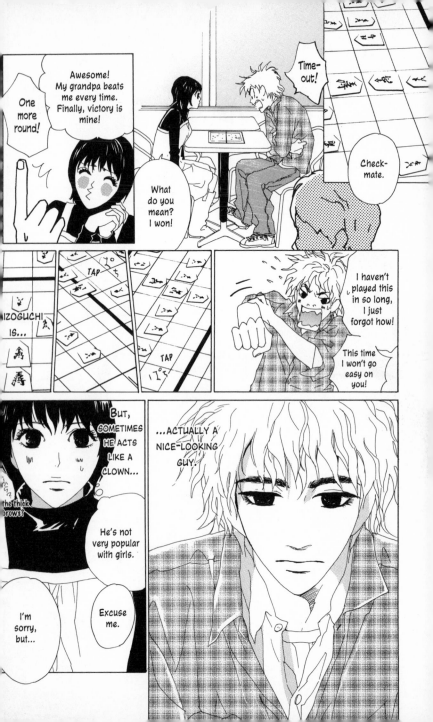

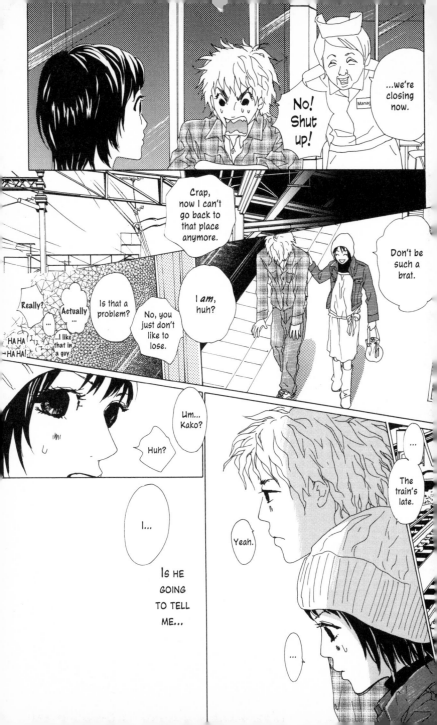

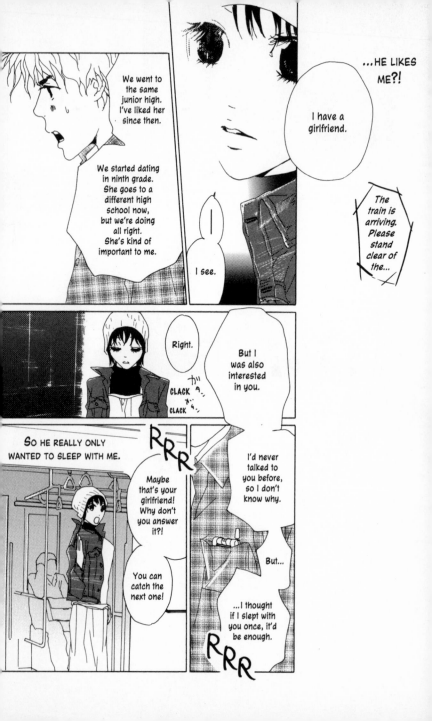

...HE LIKES ME?!

I have a girlfriend.

We went to the same junior high. I've liked her since then.

We started dating in ninth grade. She goes to a different high school now, but we're doing all right. She's kind of important to me.

I see.

The train is arriving. Please stand clear of the...

Right.

But I was also interested in you.

CLACK
CLACK

SO HE REALLY ONLY WANTED TO SLEEP WITH ME.

RRR

I'd never talked to you before, so I don't know why.

Maybe that's your girlfriend! Why don't you answer it?!

You can catch the next one!

But...

...I thought if I slept with you once, it'd be enough.

RRR

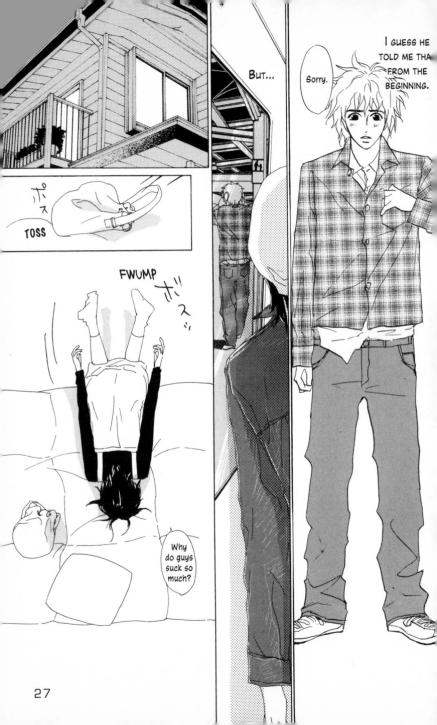

TOSS

FWUMP

Why do guys suck so much?

But...

Sorry.

I GUESS HE TOLD ME THAT FROM THE BEGINNING.

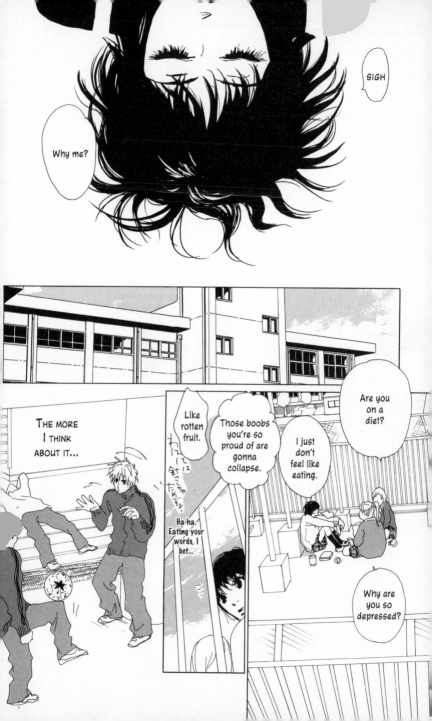

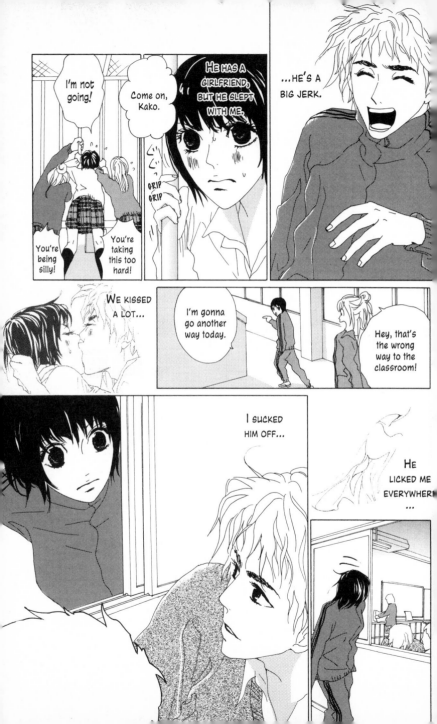

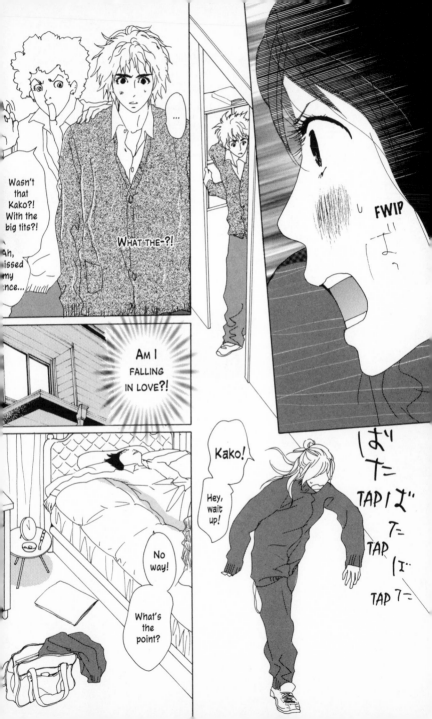

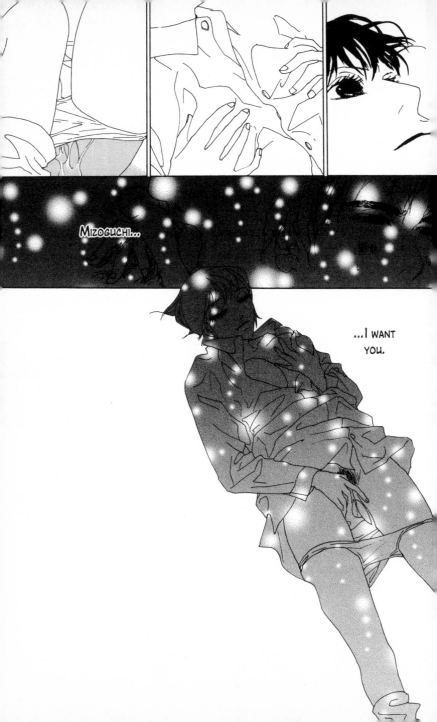

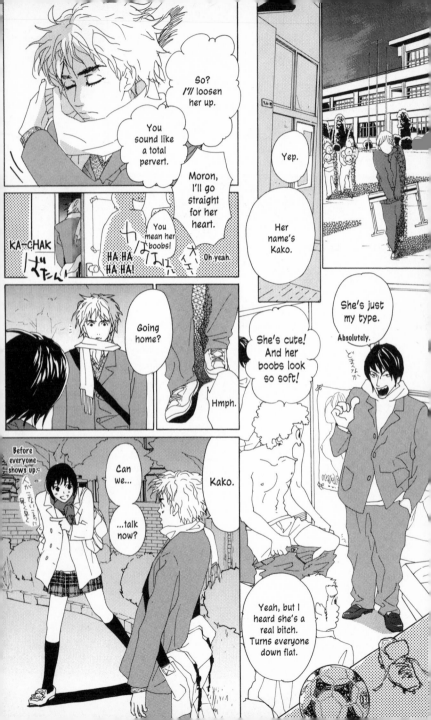

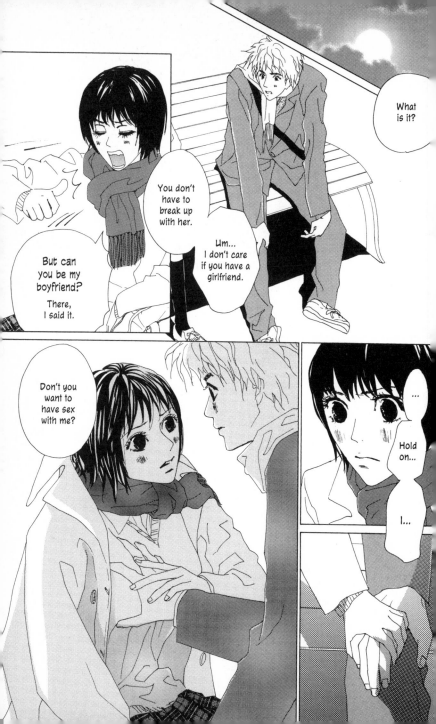

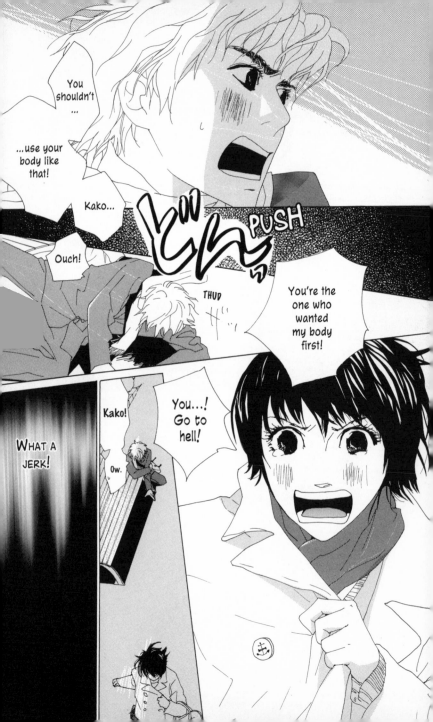

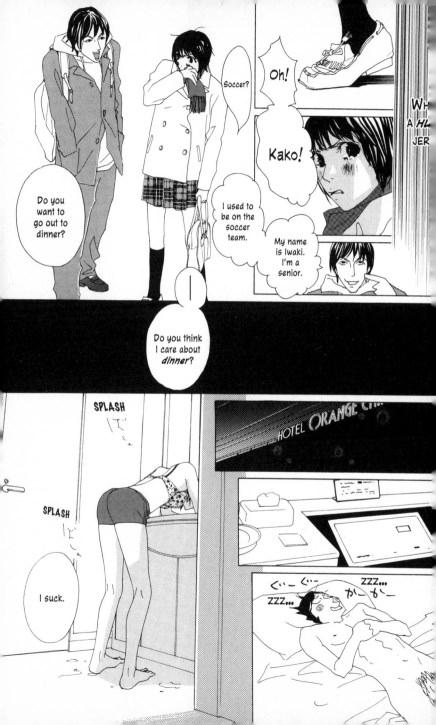

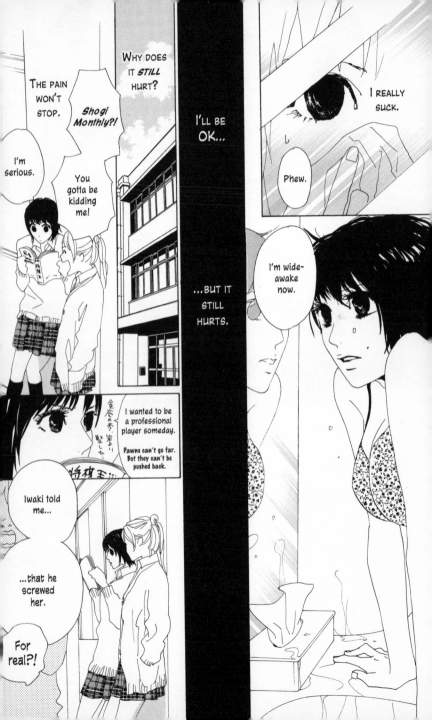

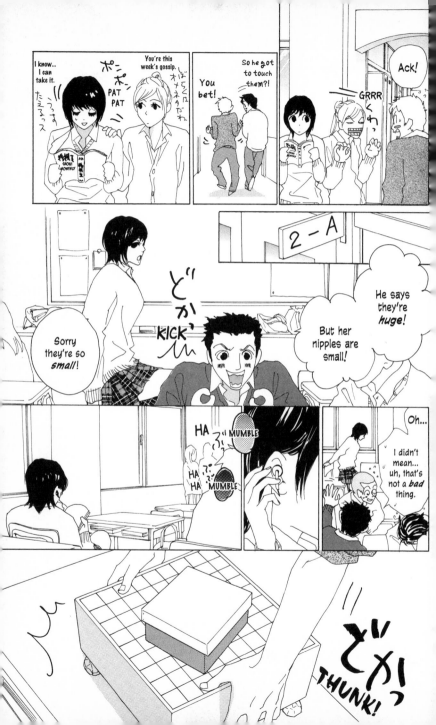

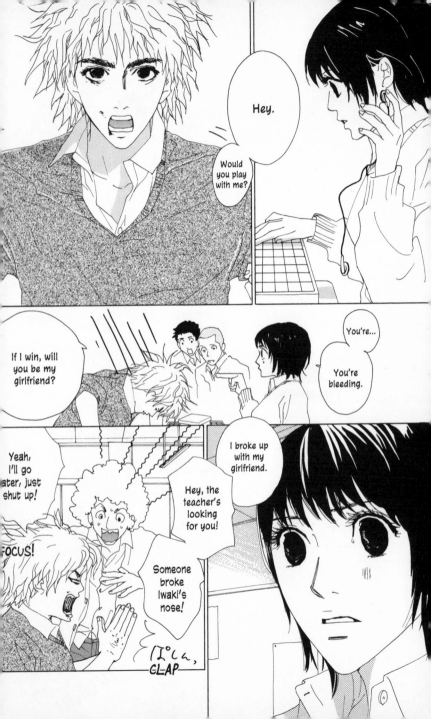

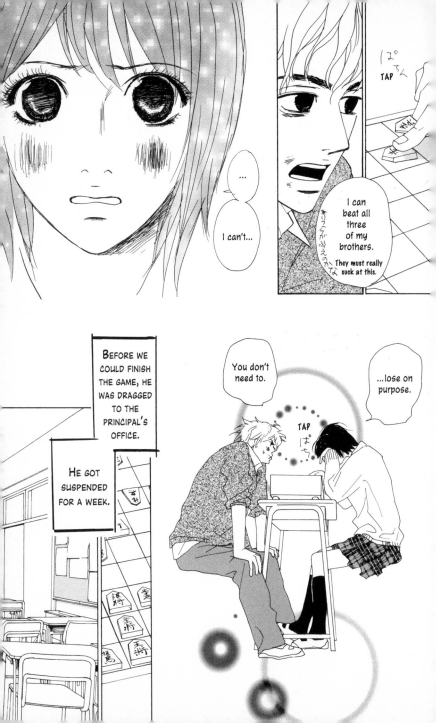

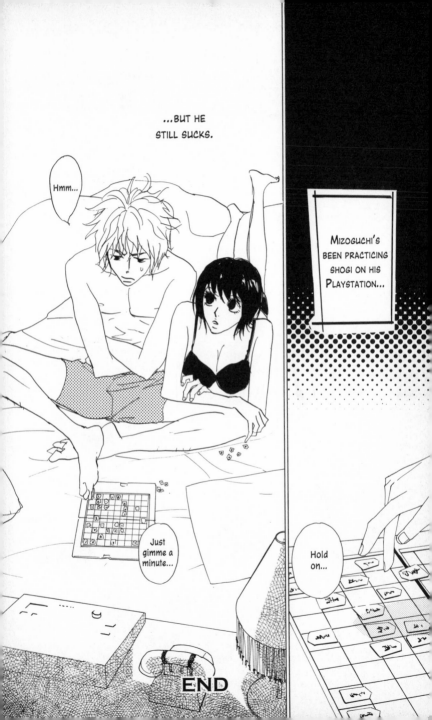

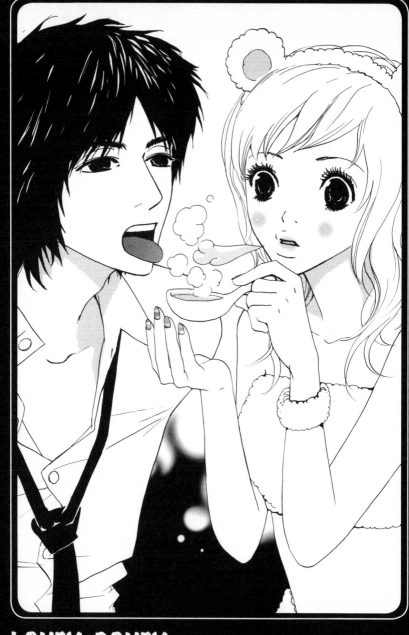

LOVEY-DOVEY

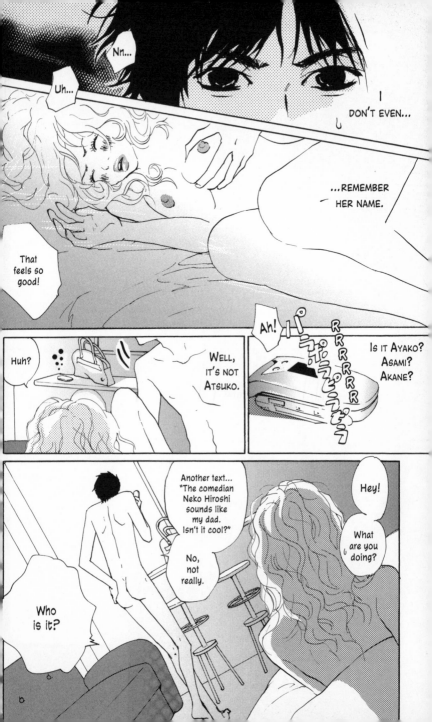

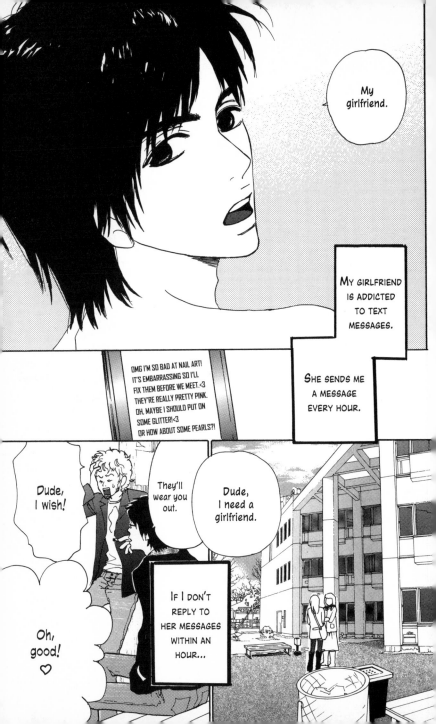

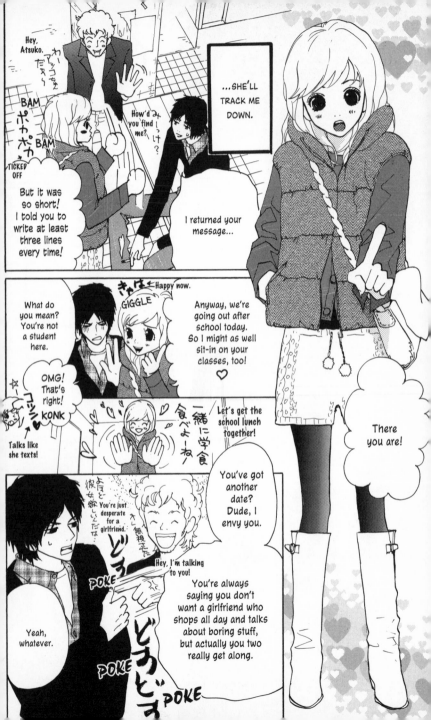

I like you. Will you be my boyfriend? ♡

Because I'm tall and good-looking...

...I don't have any trouble getting girls.

I don't care if she's a little clingy.

It's not a little.

ちょっとぐらいウザくてもいいじゃねえよ

Dude, why don't you break up with her?

I don't mind sloppy seconds!

She sent me more than twenty long messages every day. And they were about nothing.

I just erased them.

ATSUKO WAS REALLY ANNOYING BEFORE WE HOOKED UP.

知らない。
I don't know even you.

Sorry.

Can we be friends then?

Give me your e-mail address!

よろしくお願いしまああす♡

I'm looking forward to working with you!

似合うネ
制服がとても
The uniform really suits her.

As of today, she's working here part-time. Look after her.

SHE WAS PRACTICALLY A STALKER.

What is this, a Maid Cafe?!

45

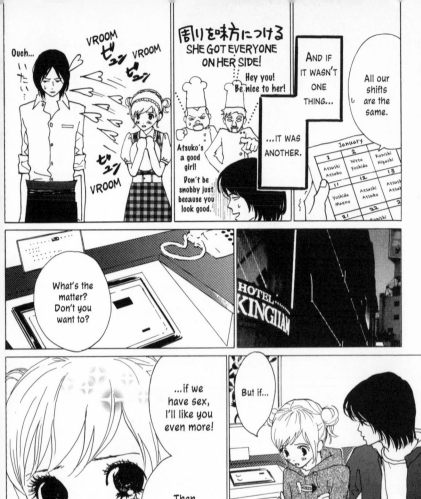

Ouch...
いた...

VROOM ビュン
VROOM ビュン
ビュン
VROOM

周りを味方につける
SHE GOT EVERYONE ON HER SIDE!

Hey you! Be nice to her!

Atsuko's a good girl!

Don't be snobby just because you look good.

AND IF IT WASN'T ONE THING...

...IT WAS ANOTHER.

All our shifts are the same.

January		
1	2	
Atsushi Atsuko	Nitta Yoshida	Konishi Higashi
11	12	13
Yoshida Maeno	Atsushi Atsuko	Atsushi Atsuk
21	22	2
	Konishi	

What's the matter? Don't you want to?

HOTEL KINGIIAN

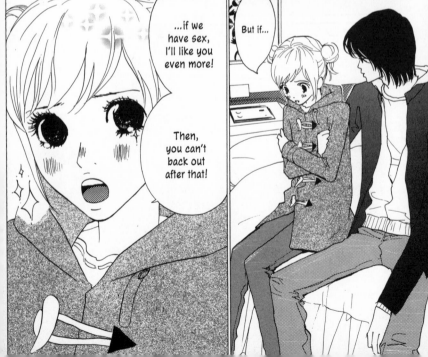

...if we have sex, I'll like you even more!

Then, you can't back out after that!

But if...

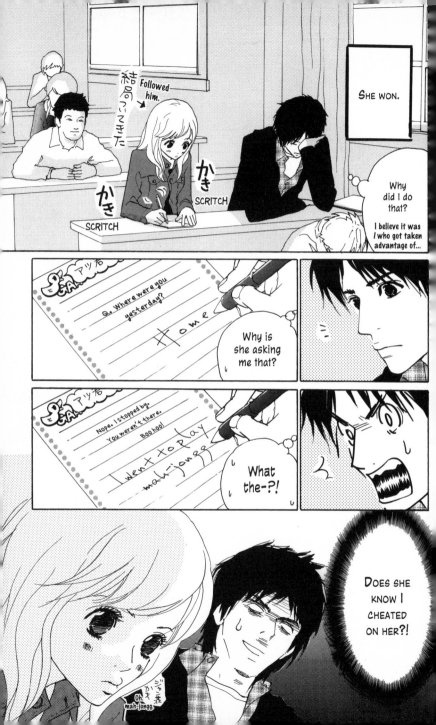

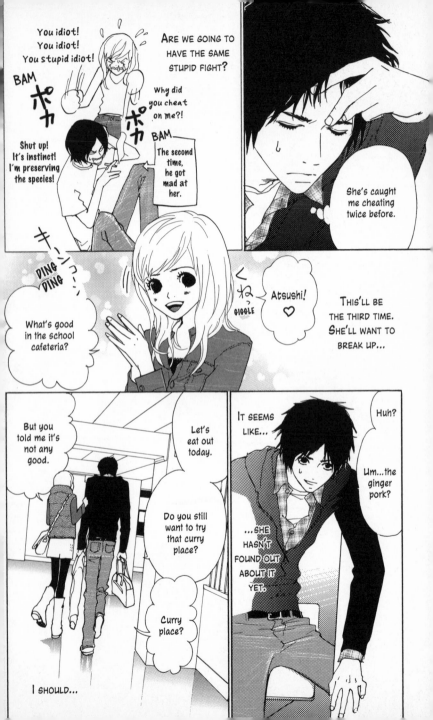

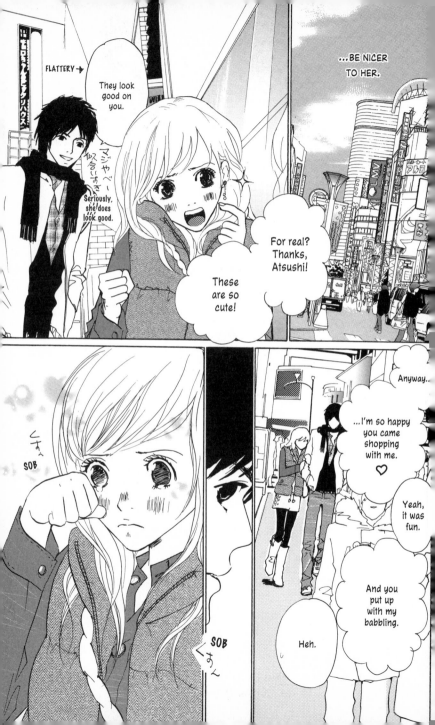

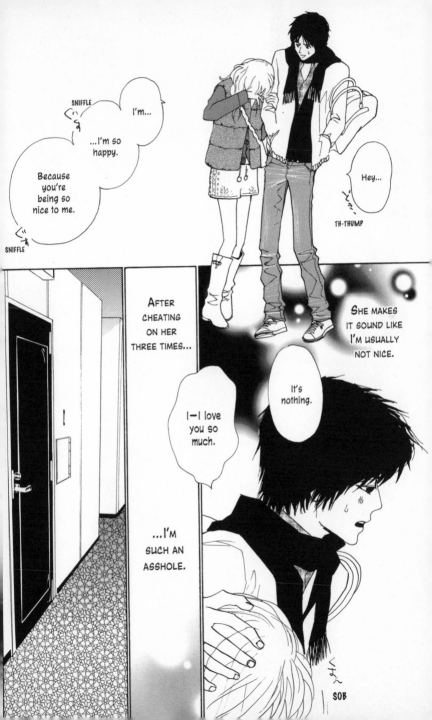

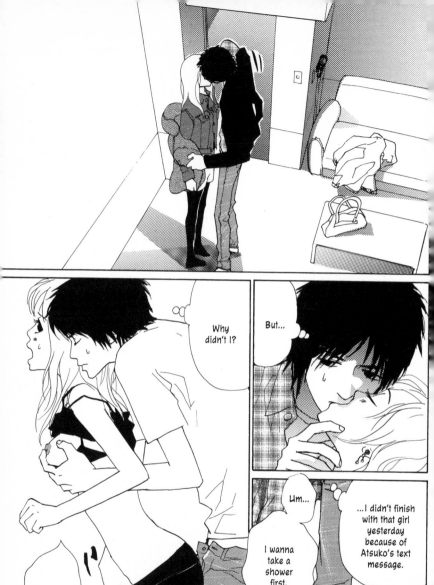

Why didn't I?

But...

Ahh... Atsushi?

Um...

I wanna take a shower first.

...I didn't finish with that girl yesterday because of Atsuko's text message.

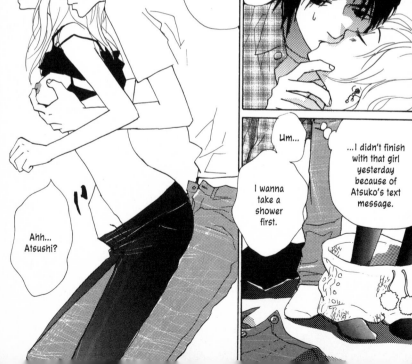

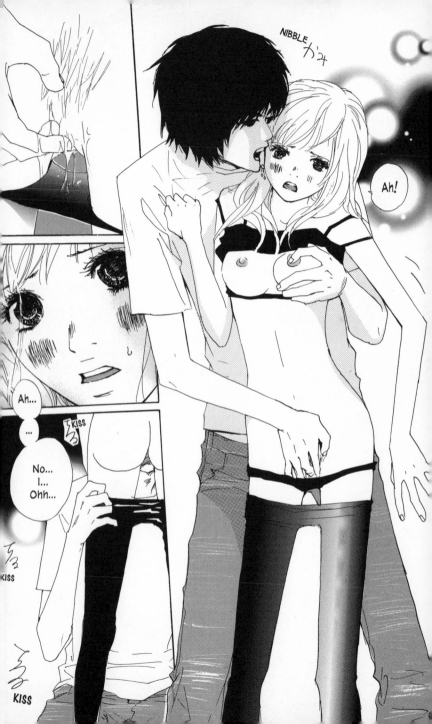

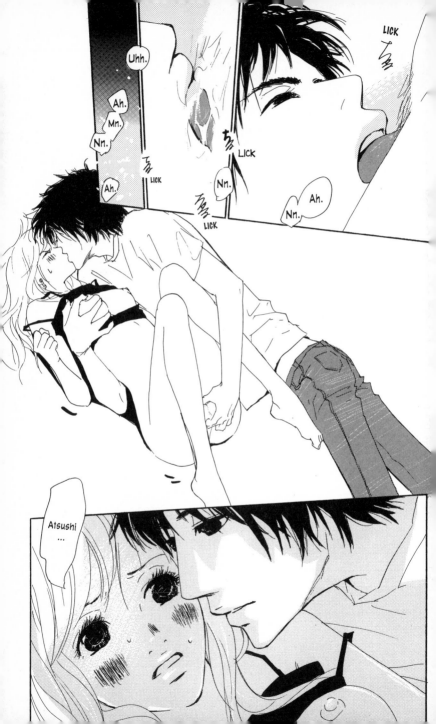

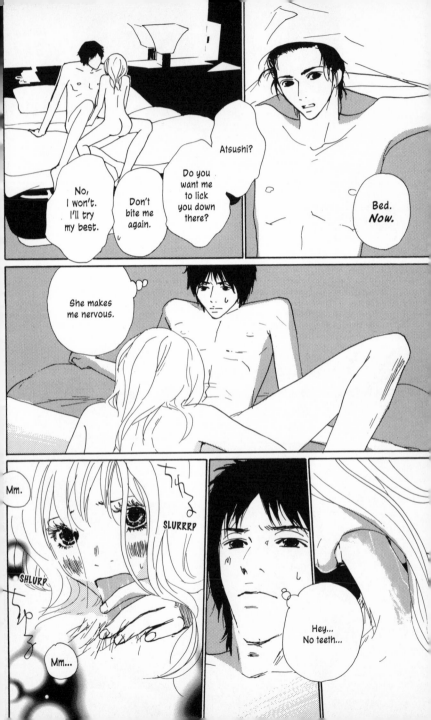

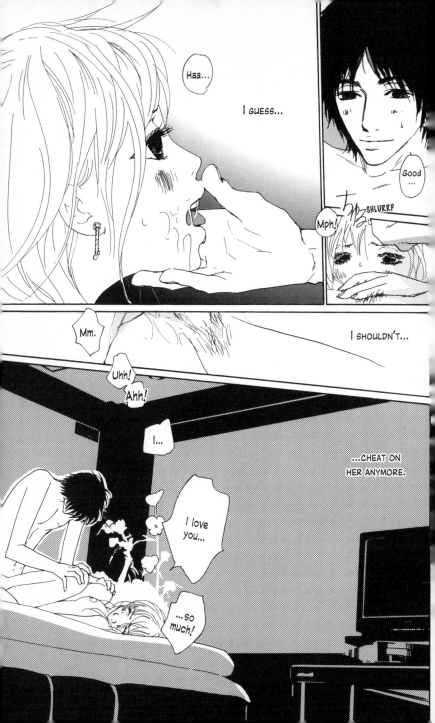

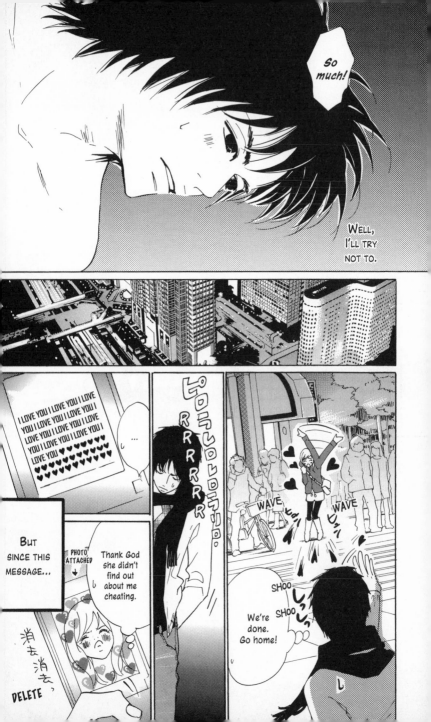

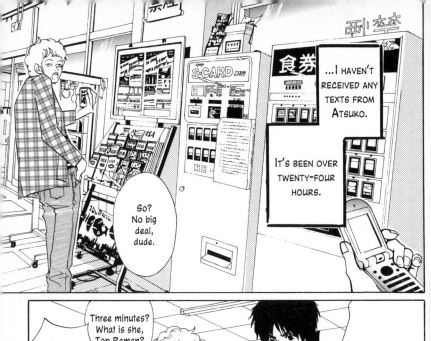

...I HAVEN'T RECEIVED ANY TEXTS FROM ATSUKO.

IT'S BEEN OVER TWENTY-FOUR HOURS.

So? No big deal, dude.

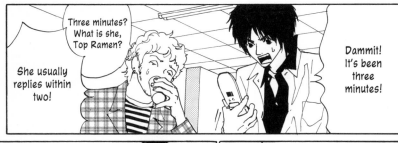

Three minutes? What is she, Top Ramen?

She usually replies within two!

Dammit! It's been three minutes!

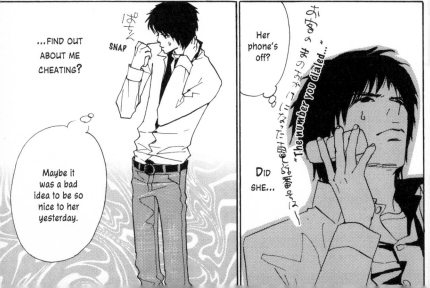

...FIND OUT ABOUT ME CHEATING?

SNAP

Maybe it was a bad idea to be so nice to her yesterday.

Her phone's off?

"The number you dialed..."

DID SHE...

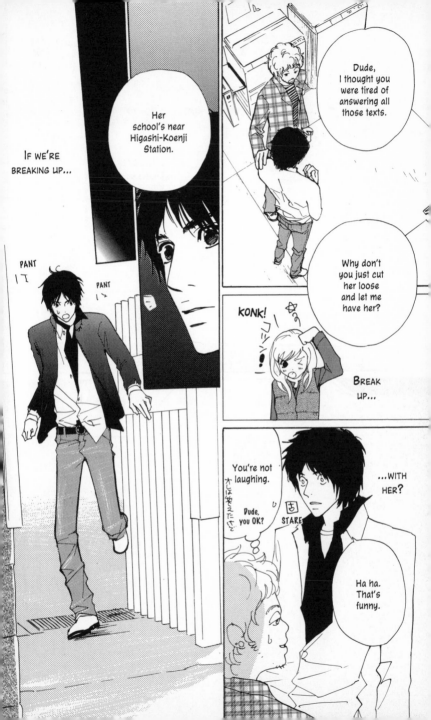

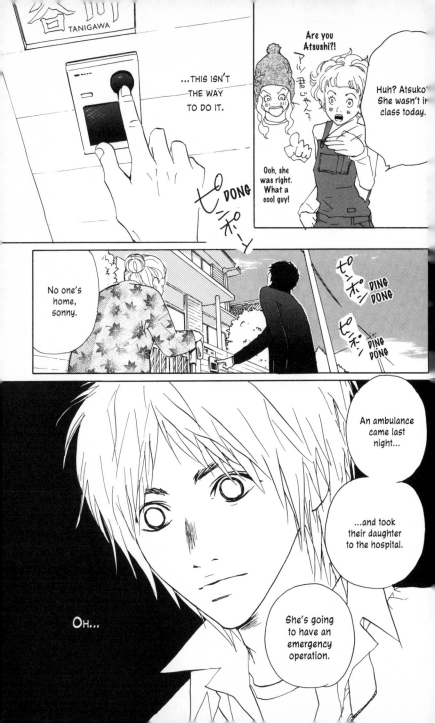

DEAR
GOD...

I'LL LISTEN TO HER TALK AND REPLY TO EVERY MESSAGE IN THREE MINUTES OR LESS!

I'LL GO SHOPPING WITH HER AND BUY HER PRESENTS!

I'LL BE NICE TO HER!

I PROMISE I'LL NEVER CHEAT ON HER AGAIN!

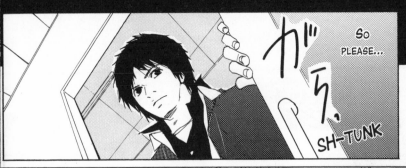

SO PLEASE...

SH-TUNK

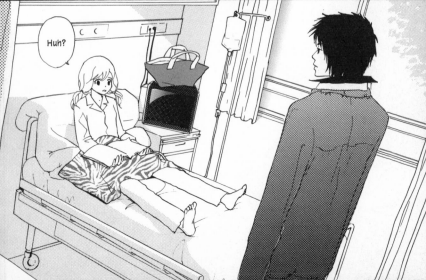

Huh?

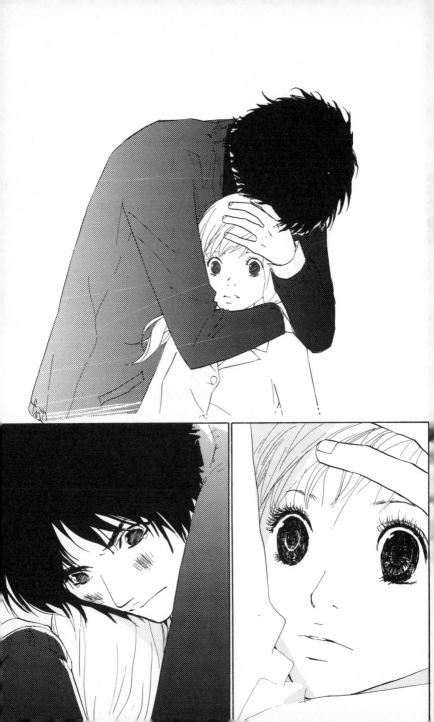

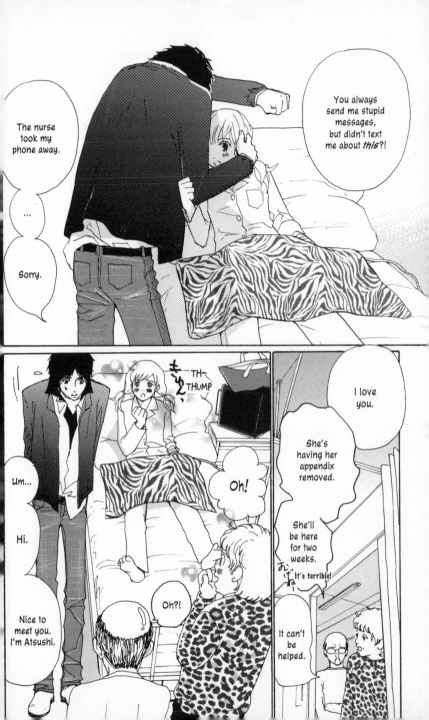

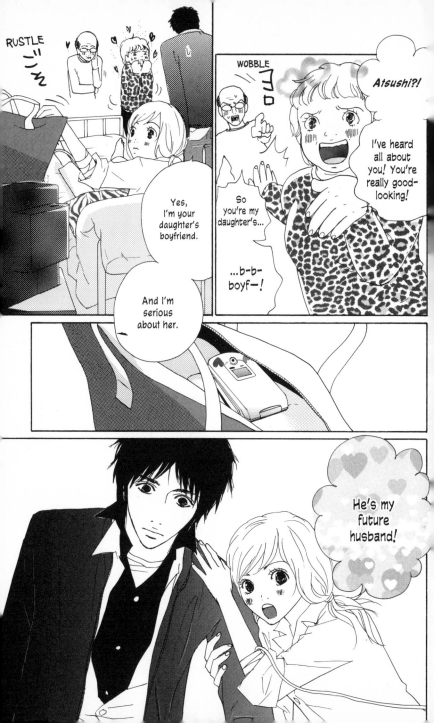

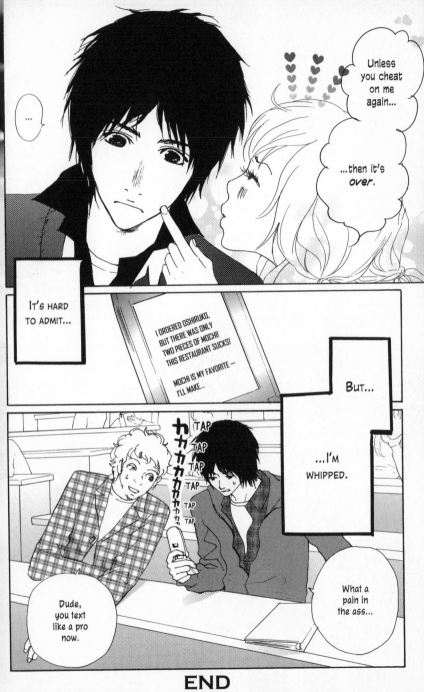

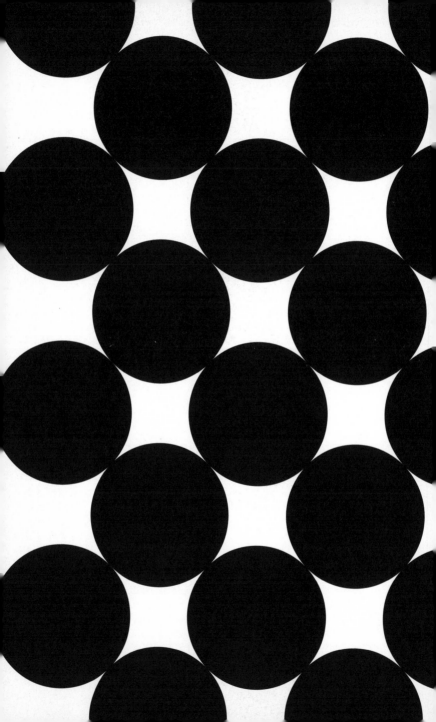

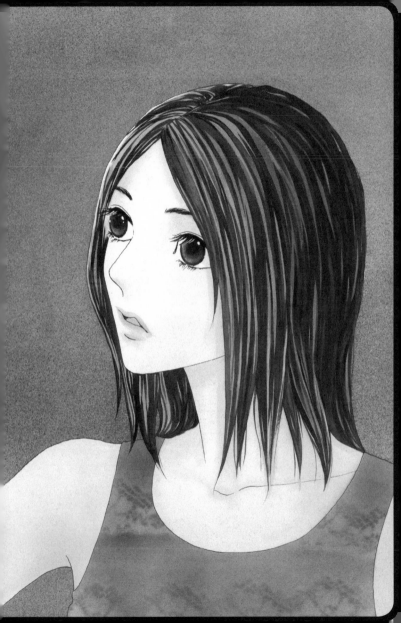

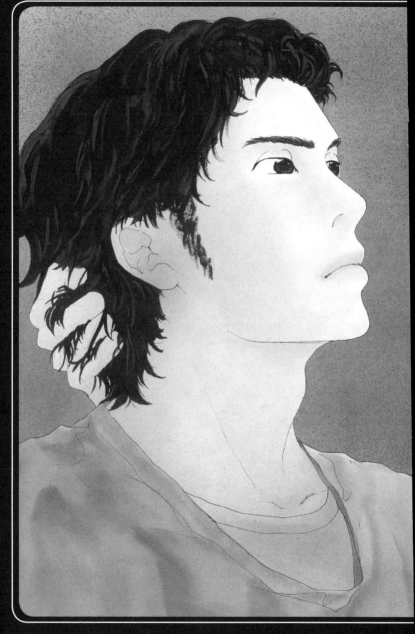

OIL & WATER

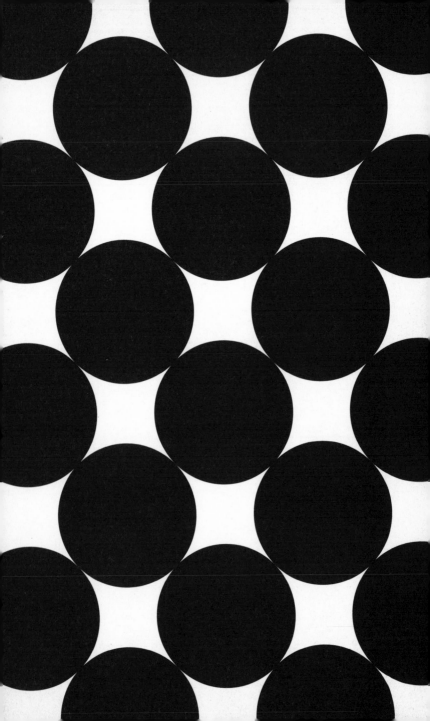

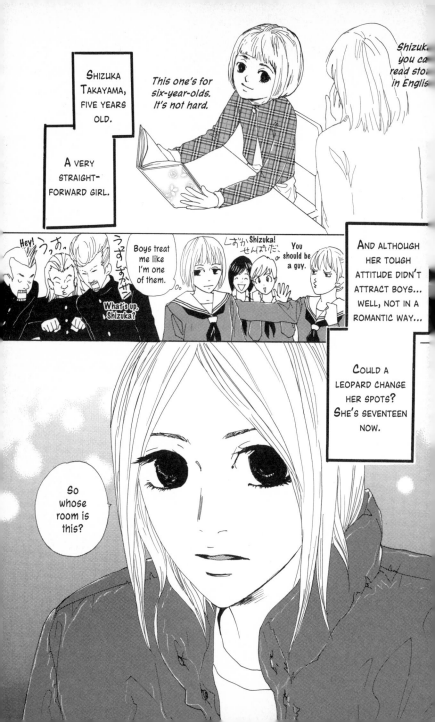

SHIZUKA TAKAYAMA, FIVE YEARS OLD.

This one's for six-year-olds. It's not hard.

Shizuk. you ca read sto in Englis

A VERY STRAIGHT-FORWARD GIRL.

Hey!

Boys treat me like I'm one of them.

What's up, Shizuka?

Shizuka! しずか せんぱいだ

You should be a guy.

AND ALTHOUGH HER TOUGH ATTITUDE DIDN'T ATTRACT BOYS... WELL, NOT IN A ROMANTIC WAY...

COULD A LEOPARD CHANGE HER SPOTS? SHE'S SEVENTEEN NOW.

So whose room is this?

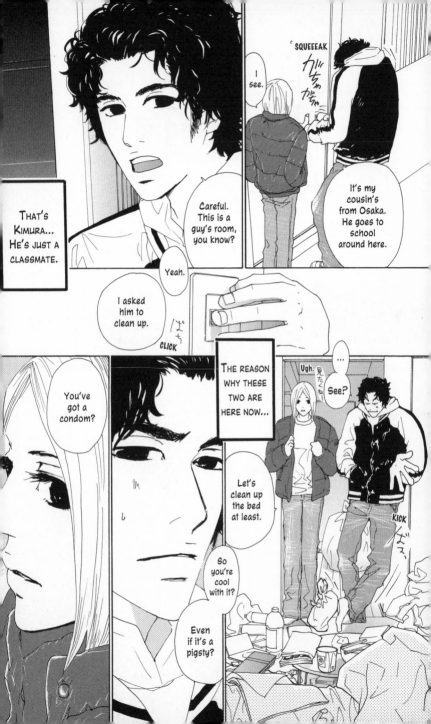

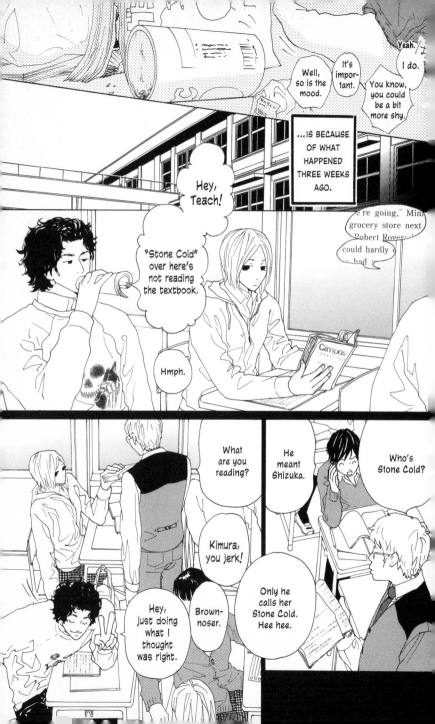

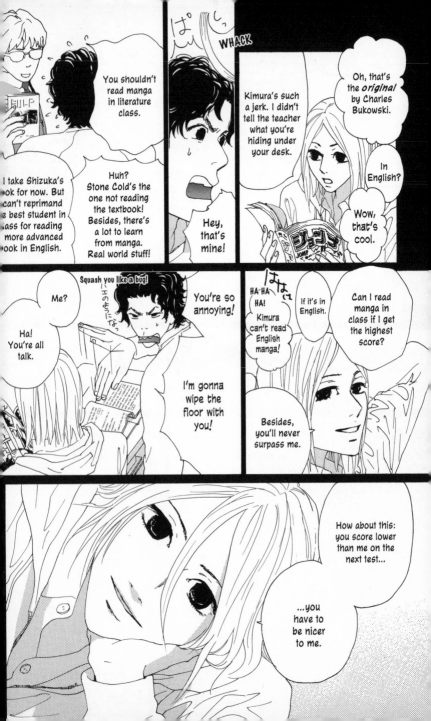

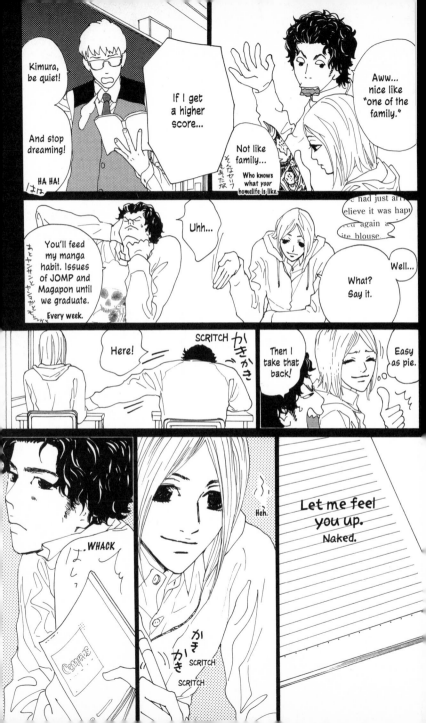

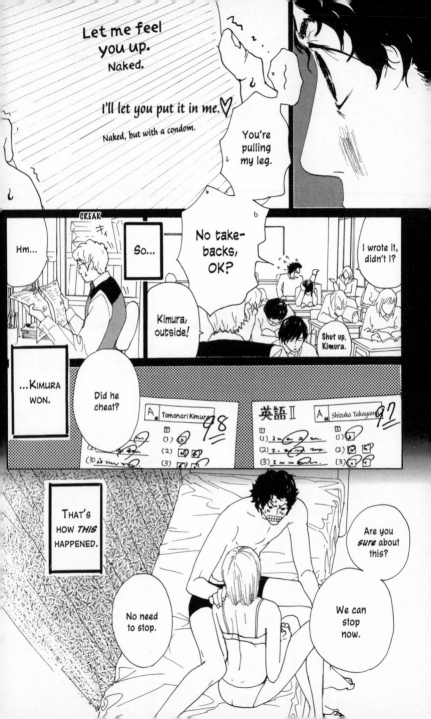

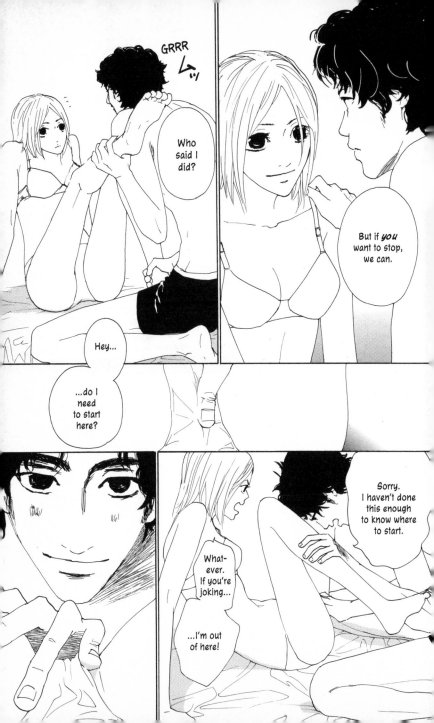

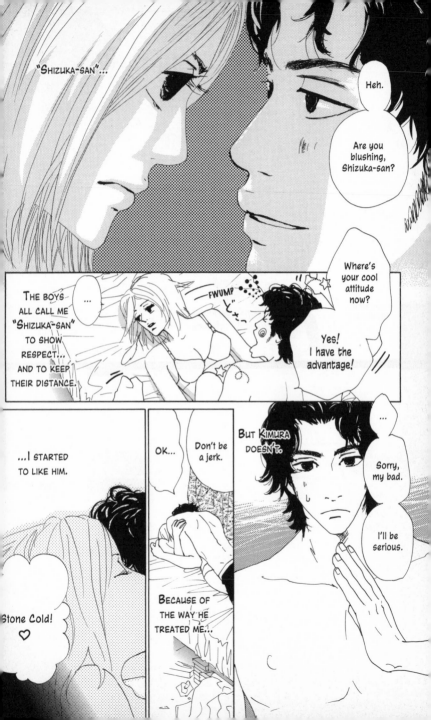

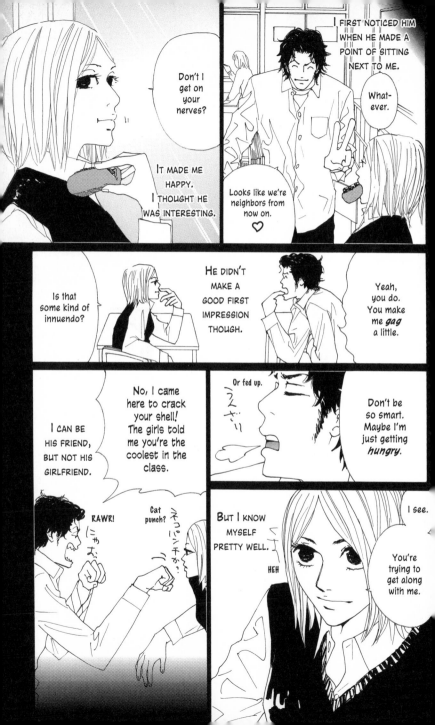

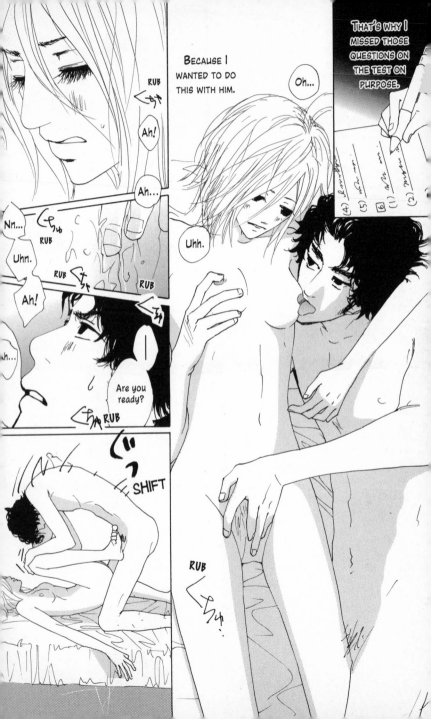

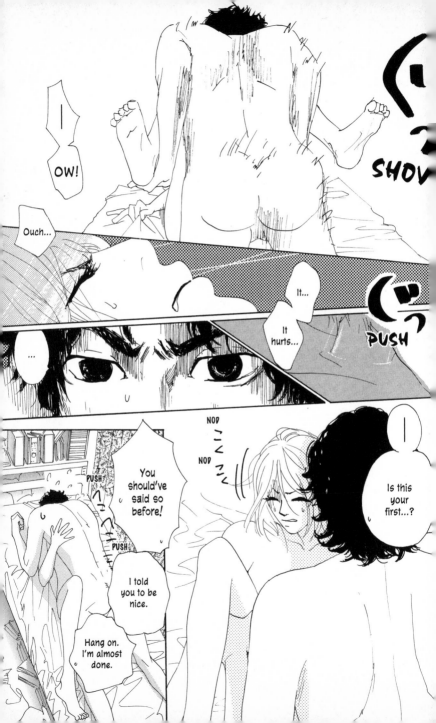

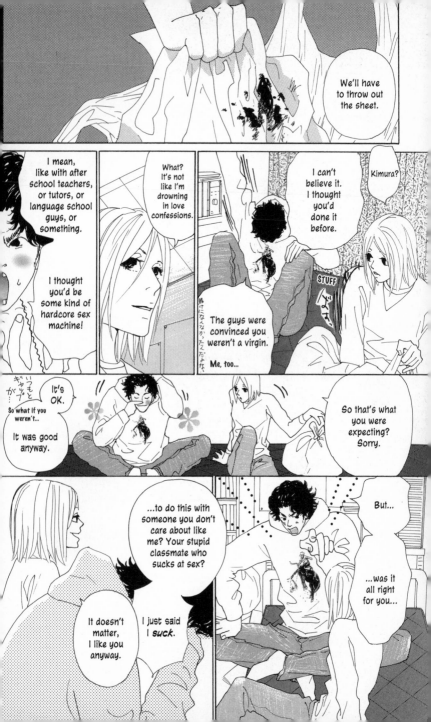

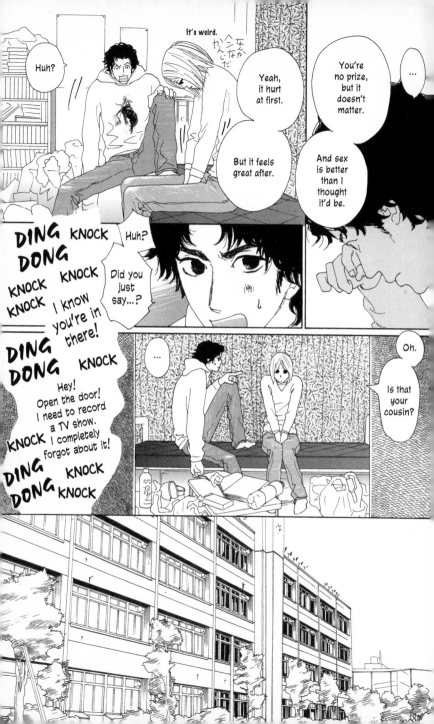

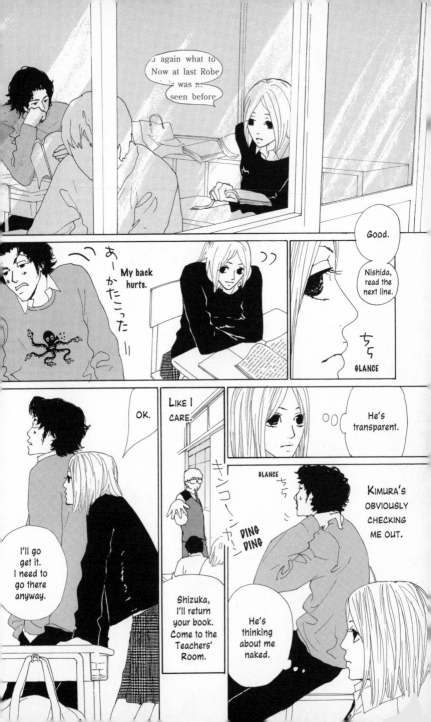

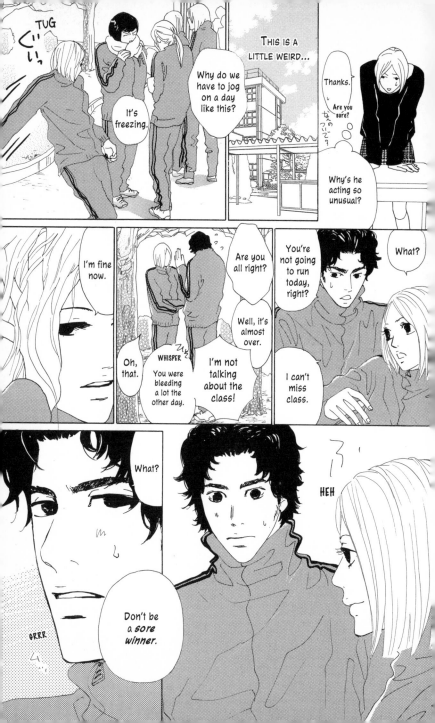

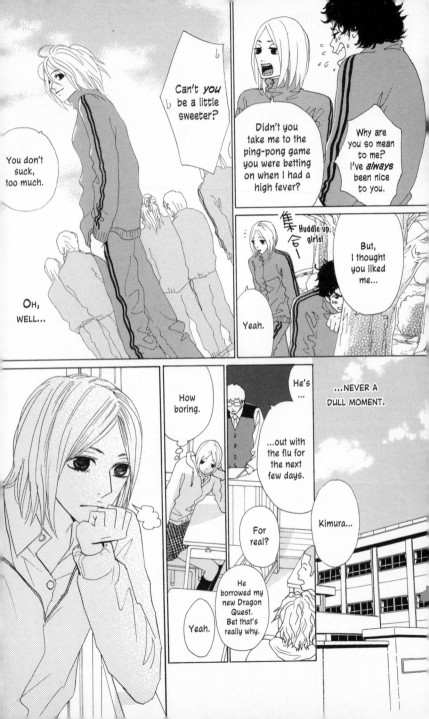

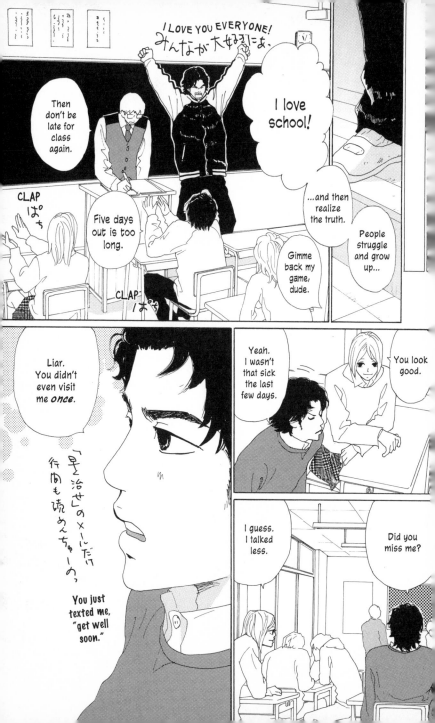

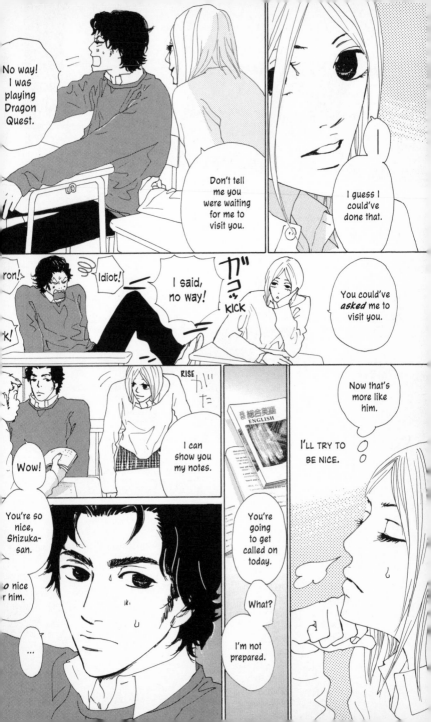

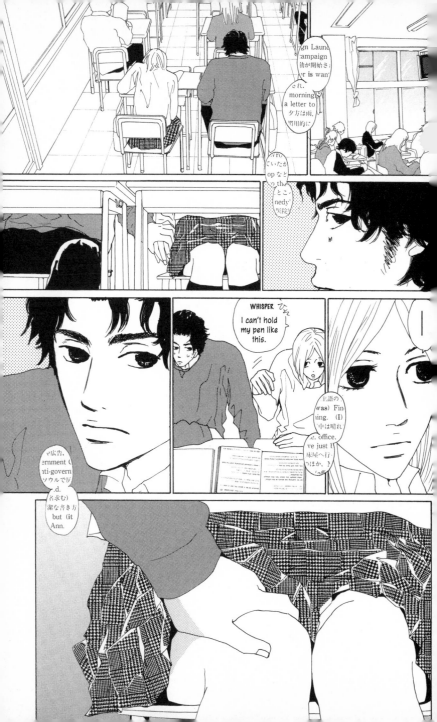

WHISPER ひそ

I can't hold my pen like this.

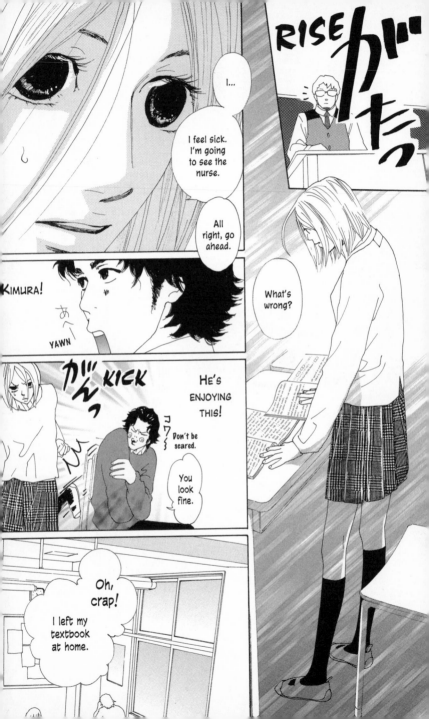

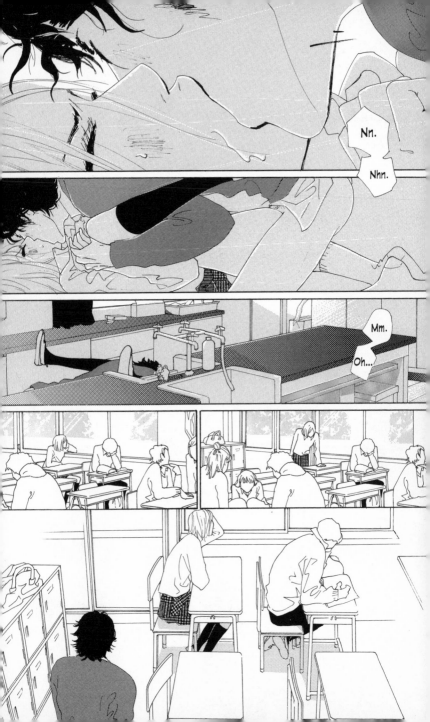

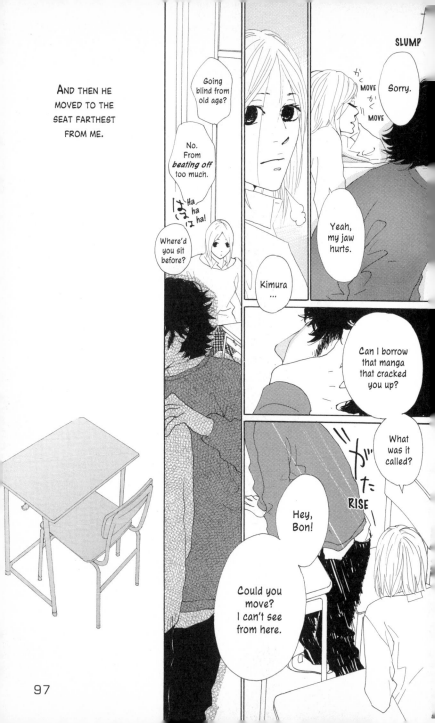

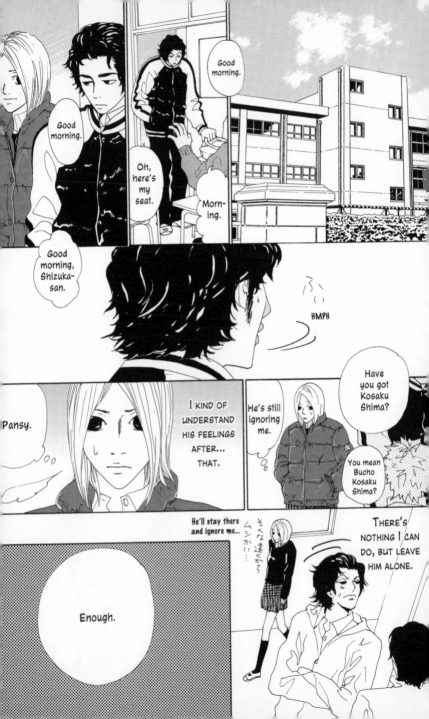

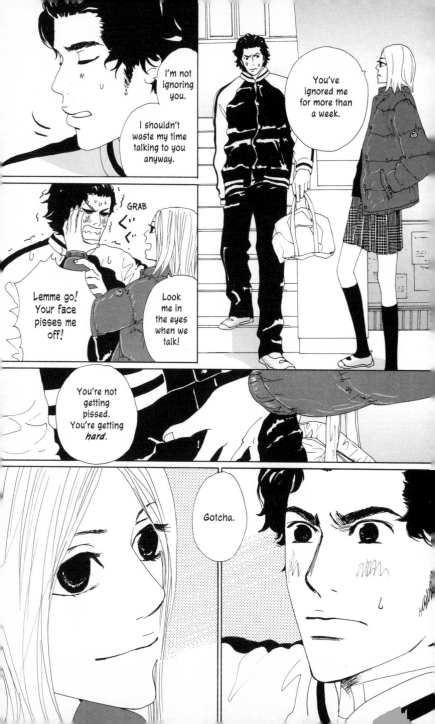

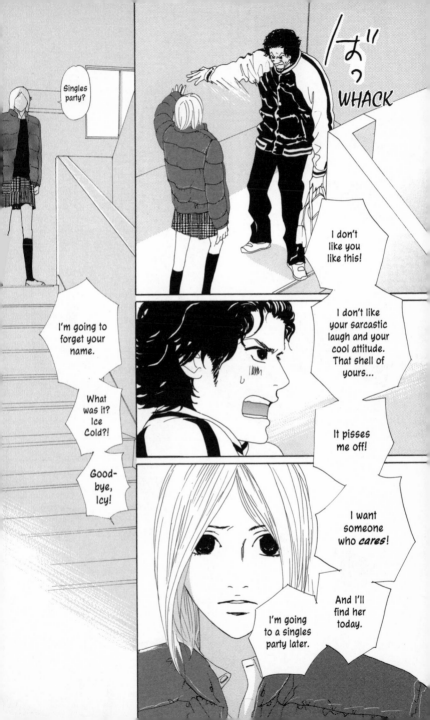

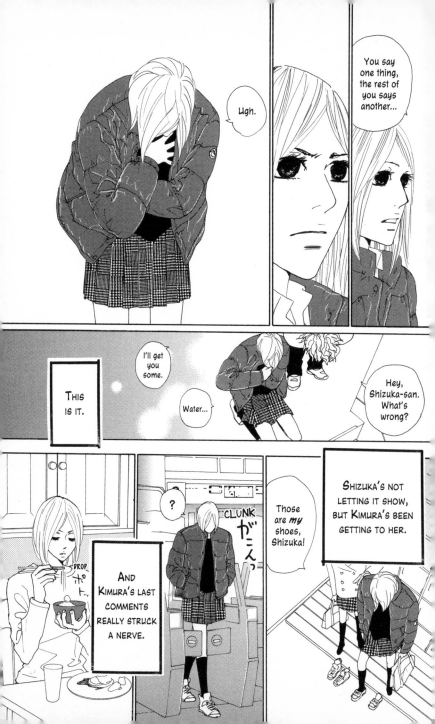

Ugh.

You say one thing, the rest of you says another...

I'll get you some.

Water...

THIS IS IT.

Hey, Shizuka-san. What's wrong?

?

CLUNK
がこん

Those are *my* shoes, Shizuka!

AND KIMURA'S LAST COMMENTS REALLY STRUCK A NERVE.

DROP
ポト…

SHIZUKA'S NOT LETTING IT SHOW, BUT KIMURA'S BEEN GETTING TO HER.

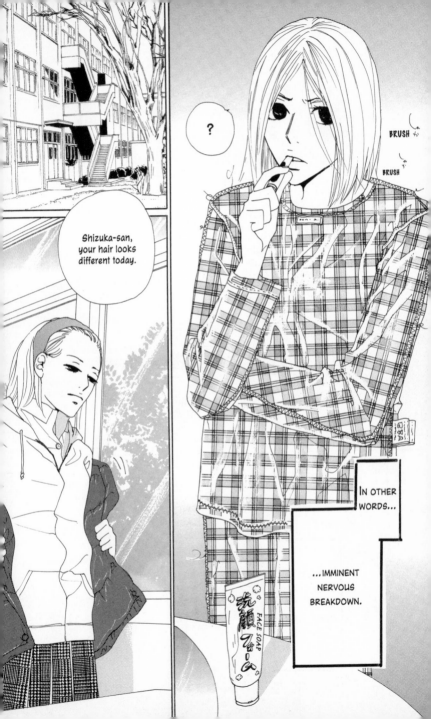

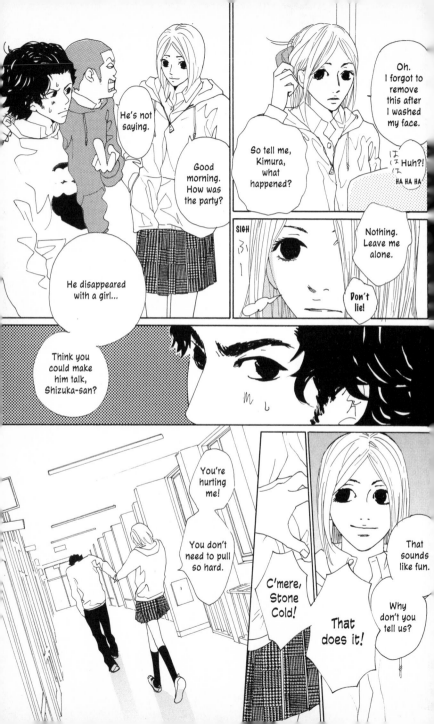

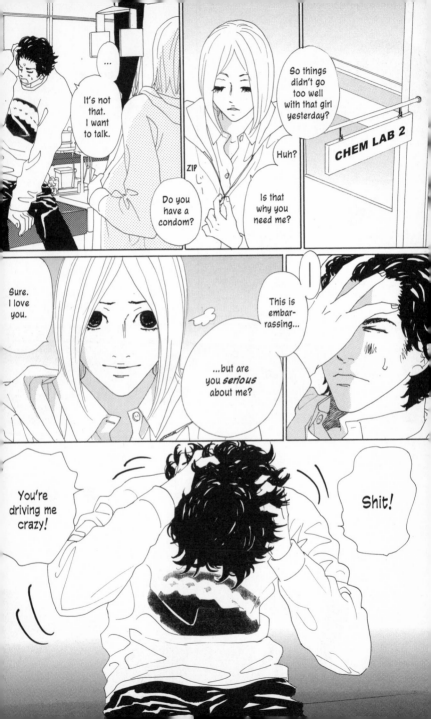

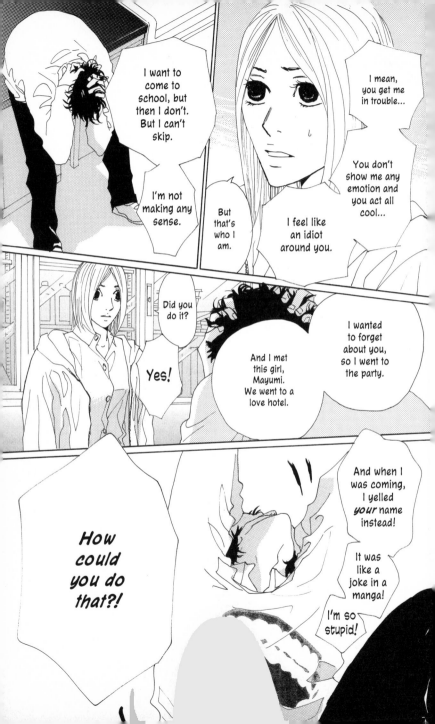

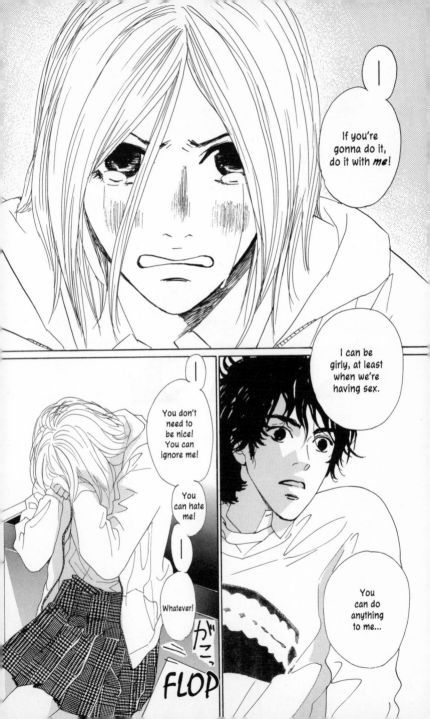

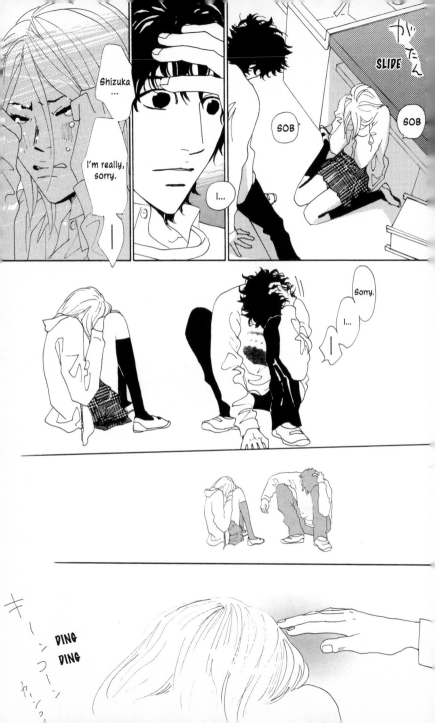

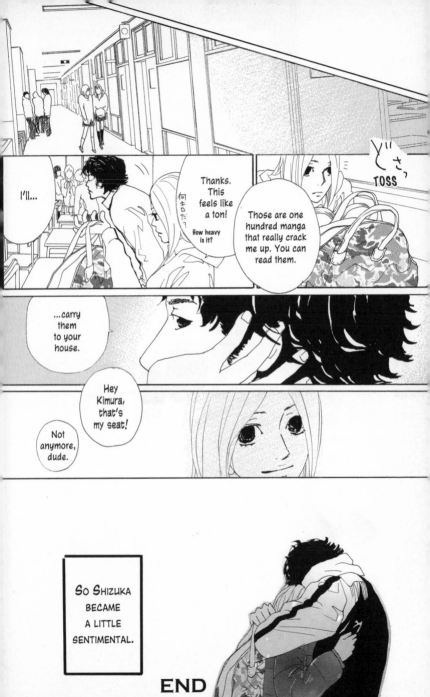

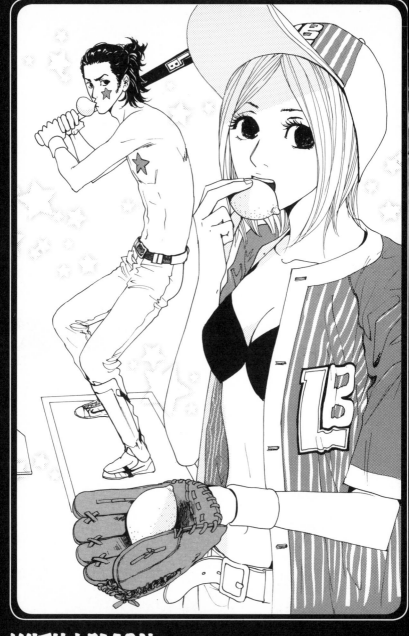

WITH LEMON

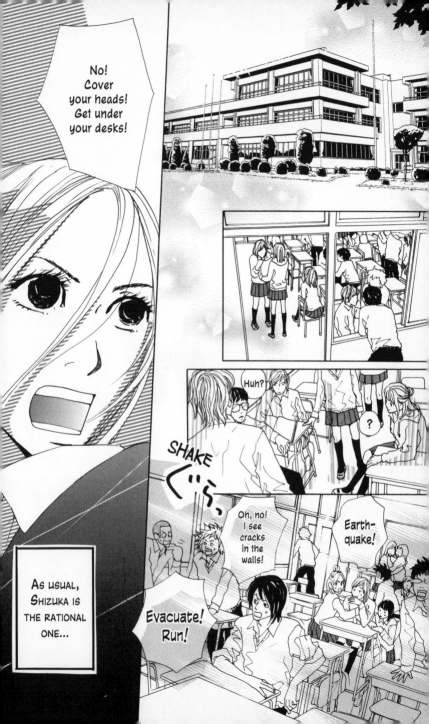

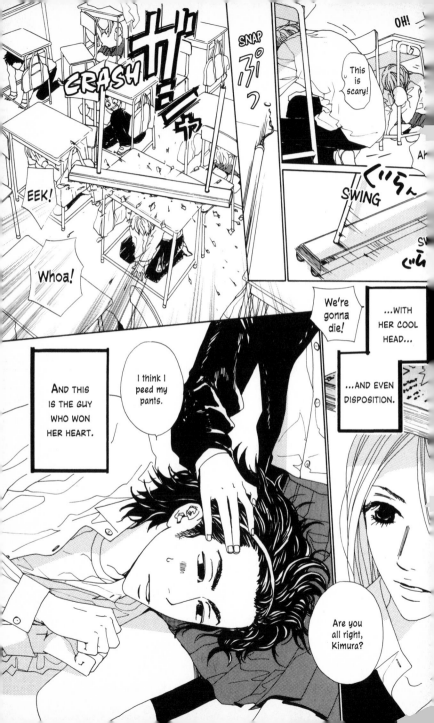

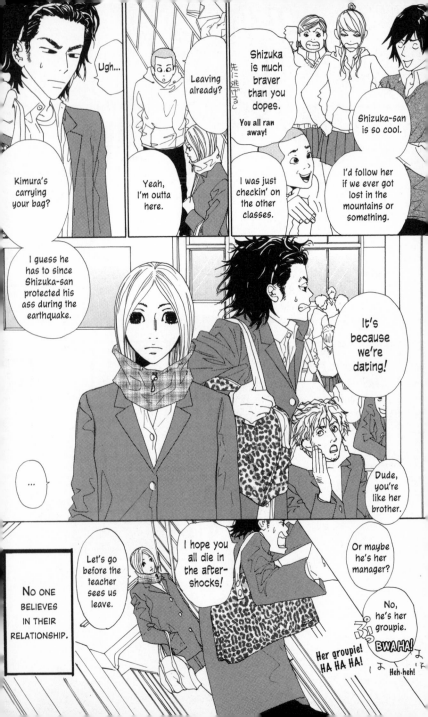

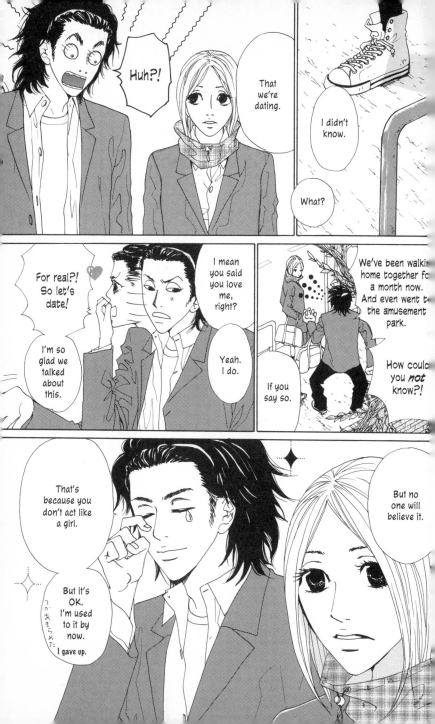

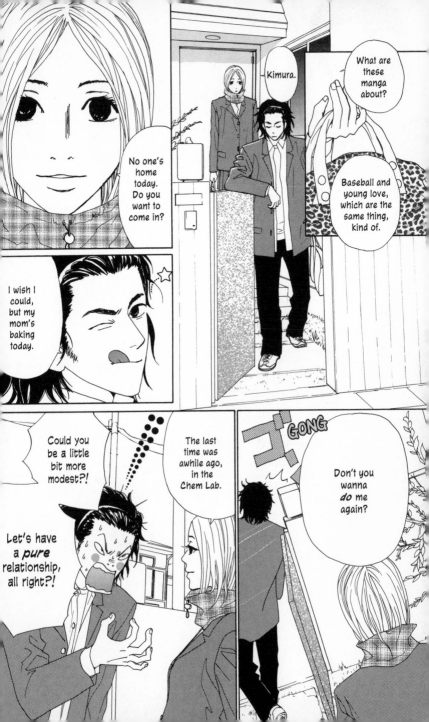

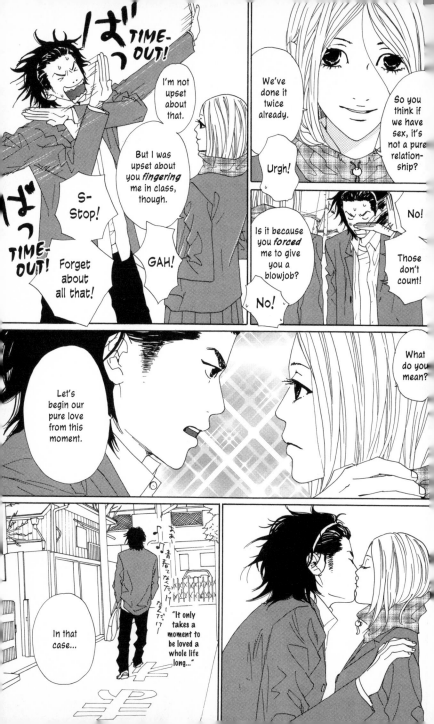

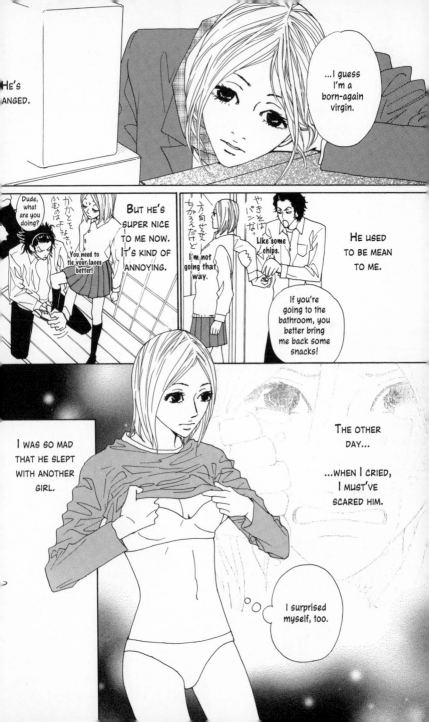

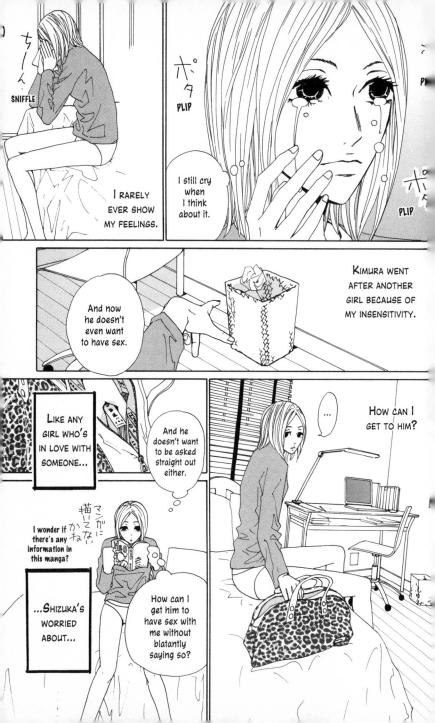

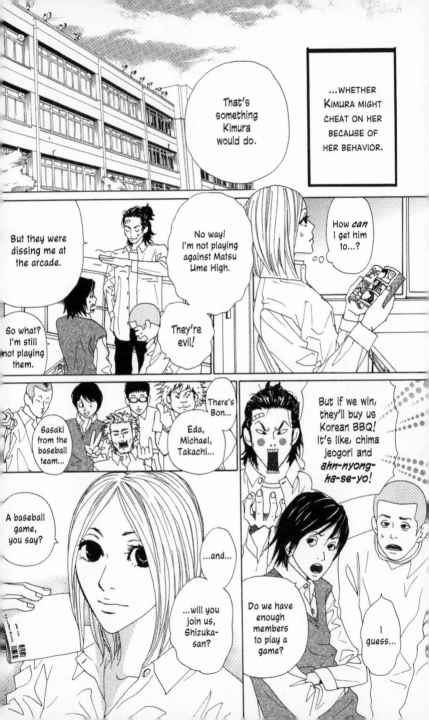

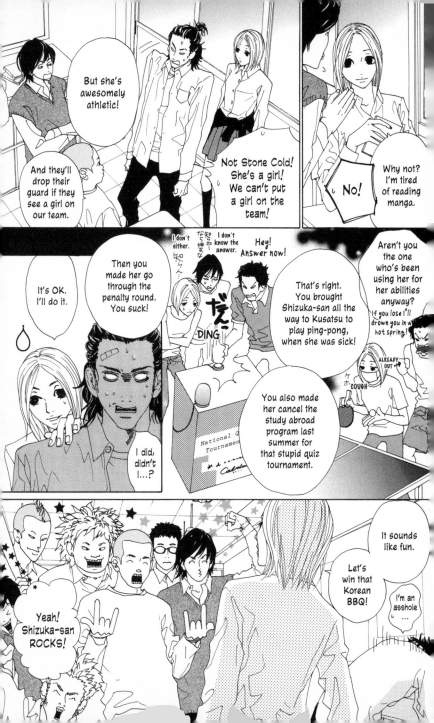

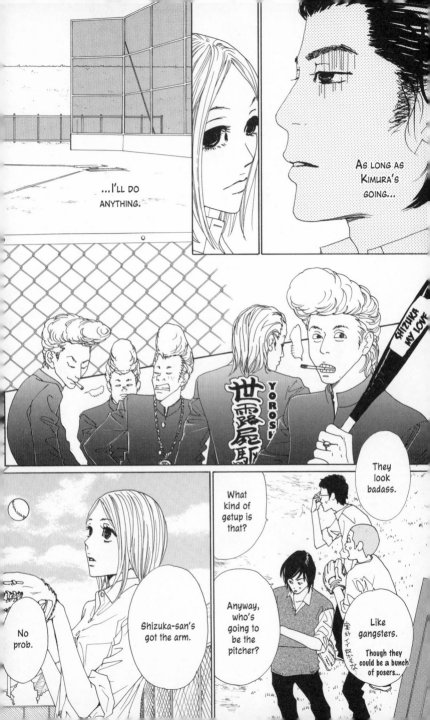

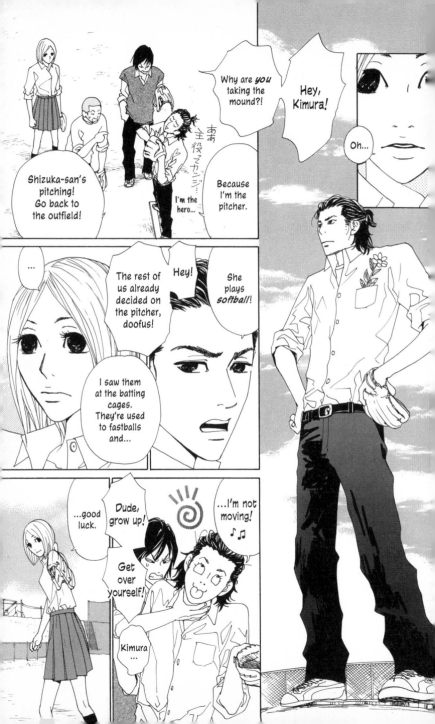

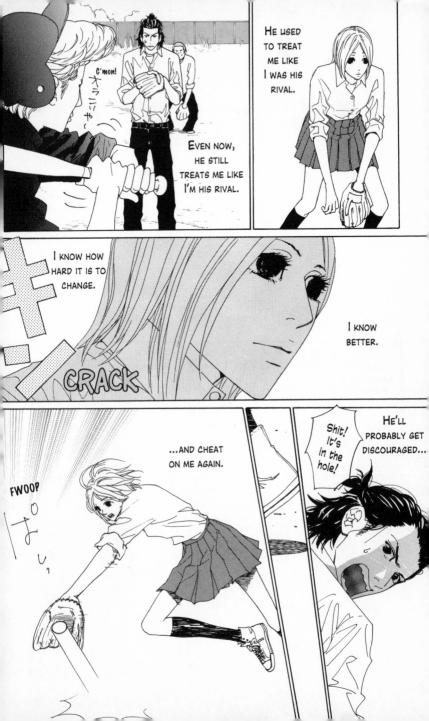

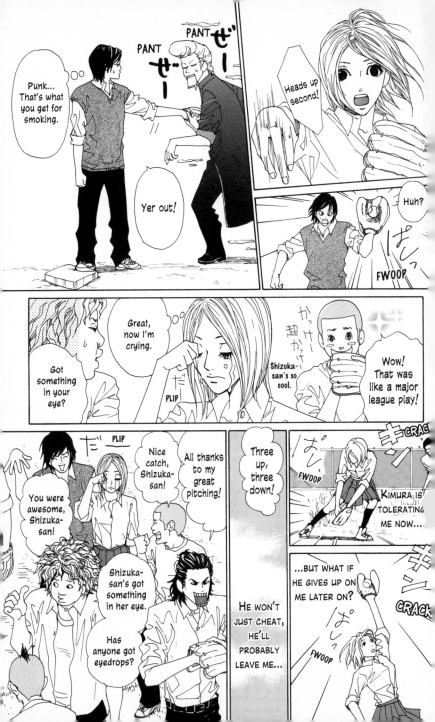

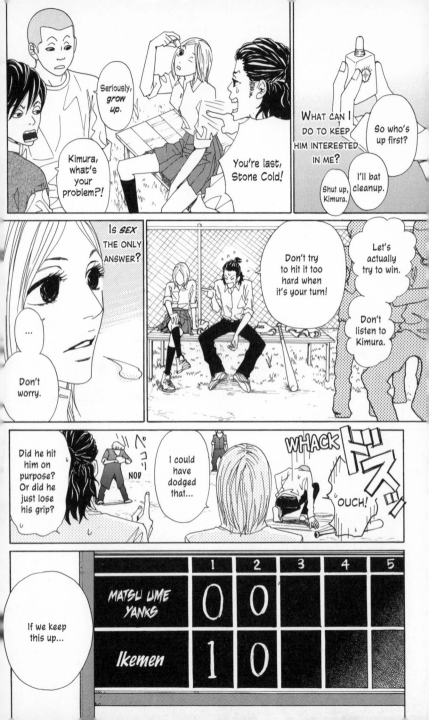

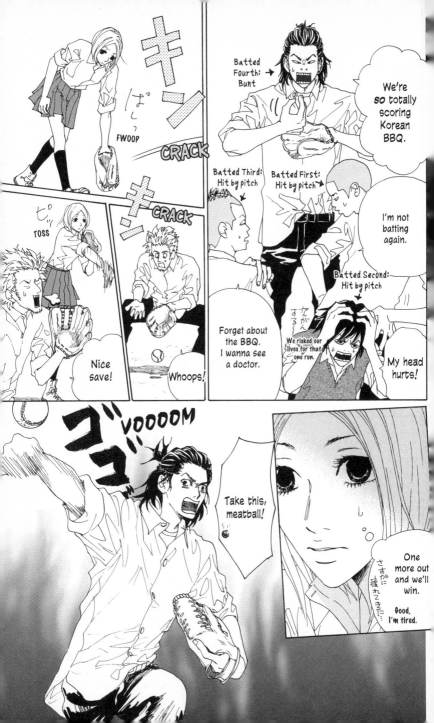

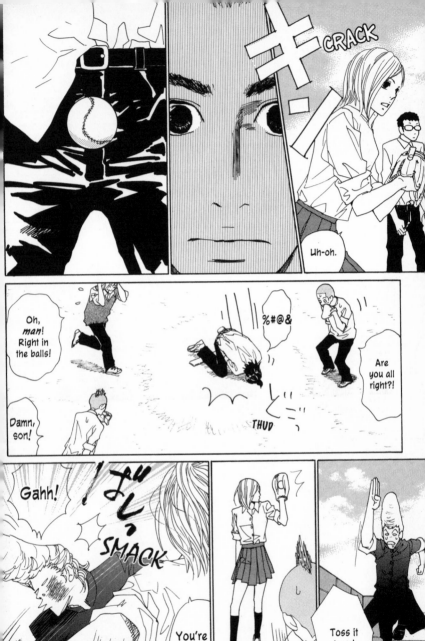
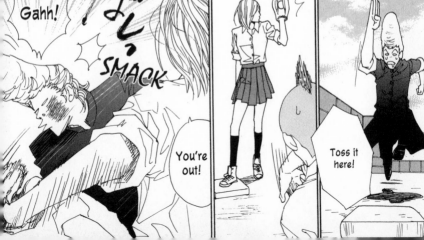

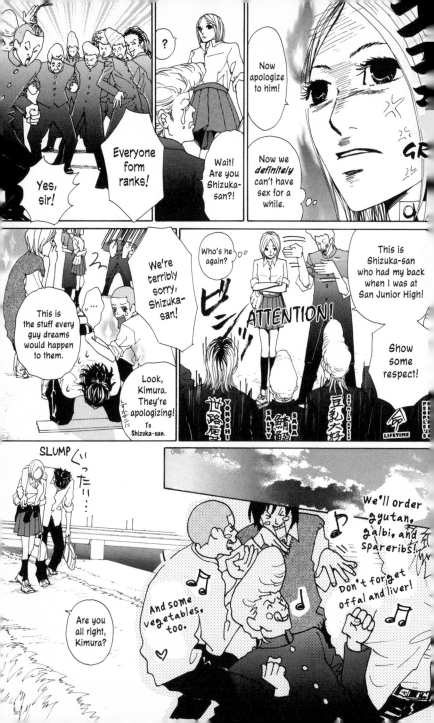

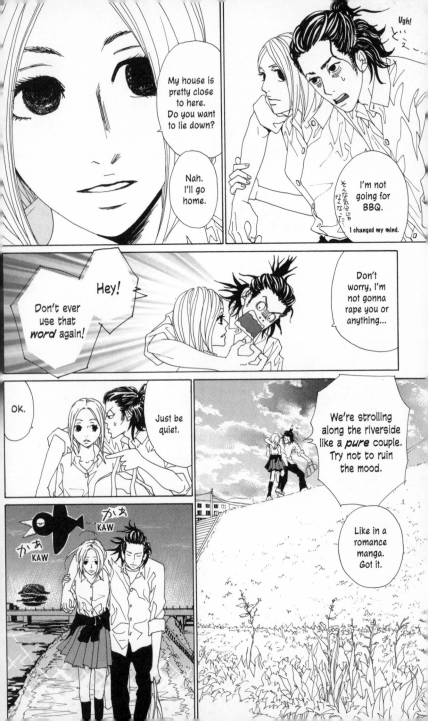

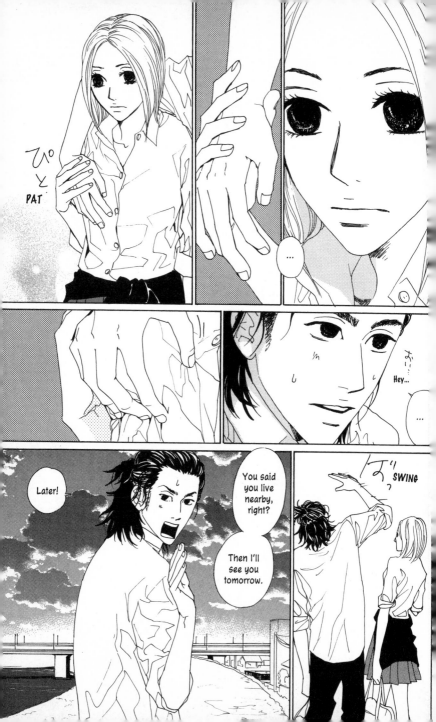

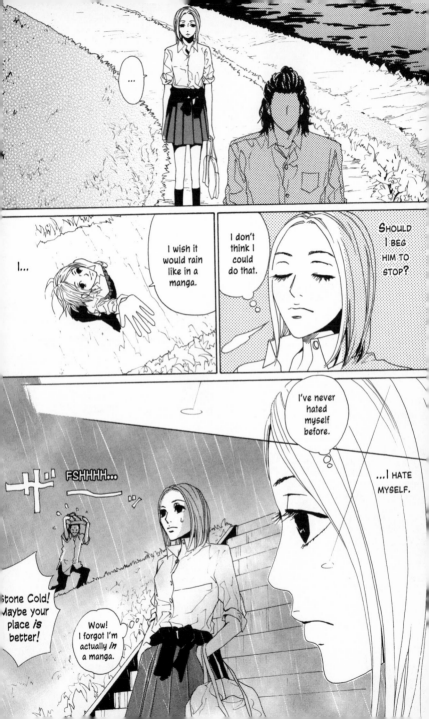

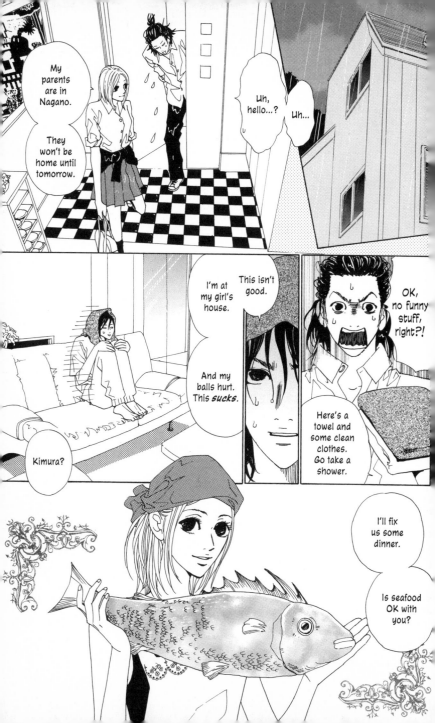

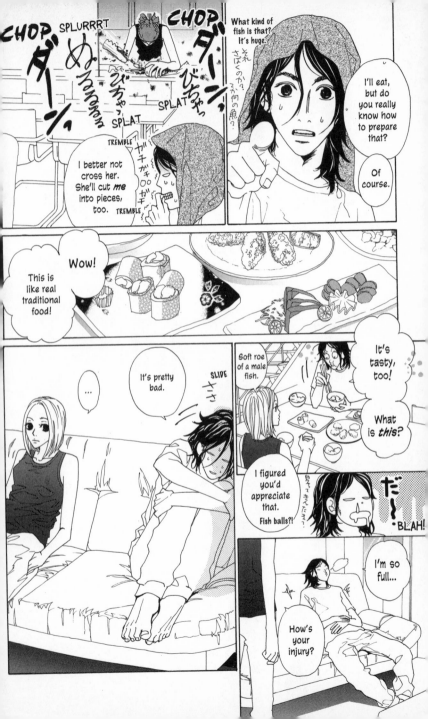

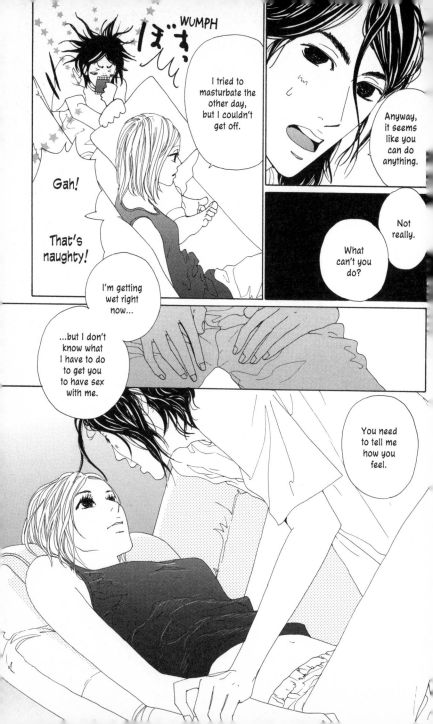

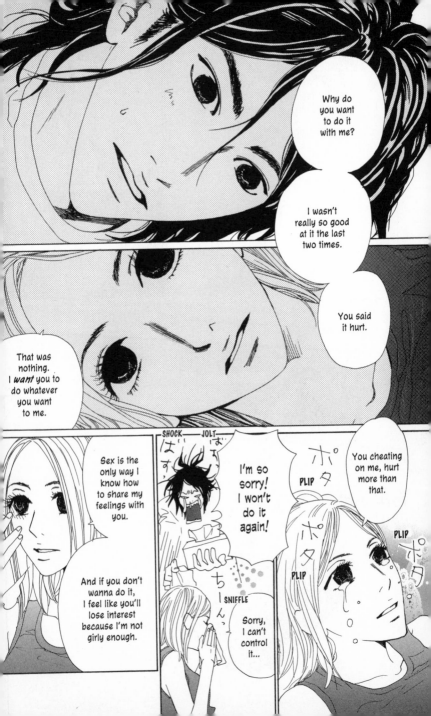

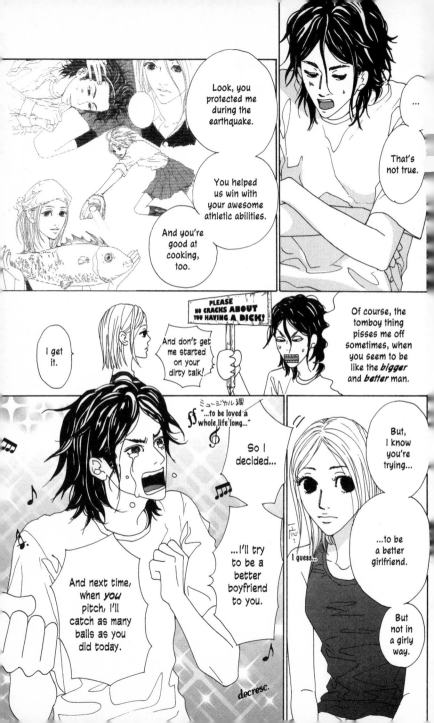

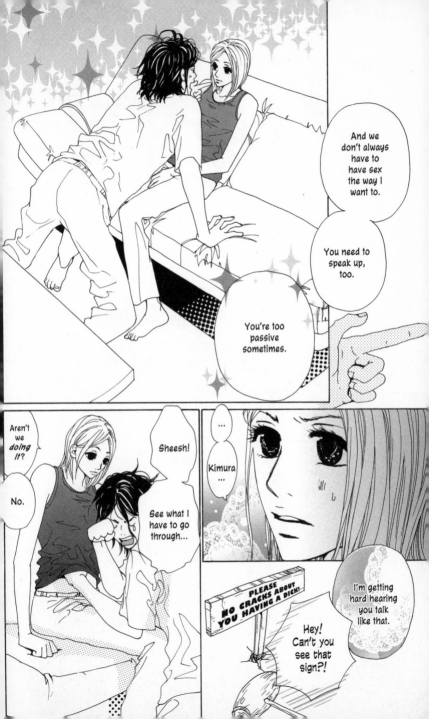

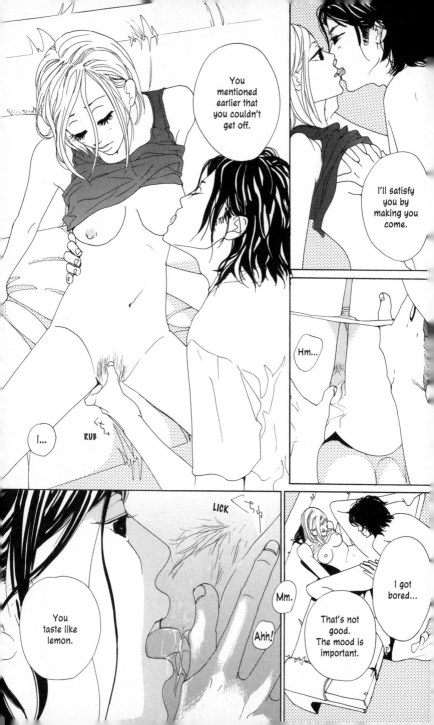

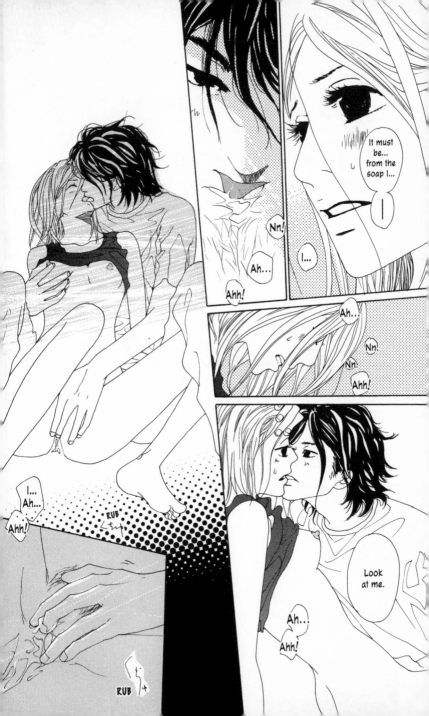

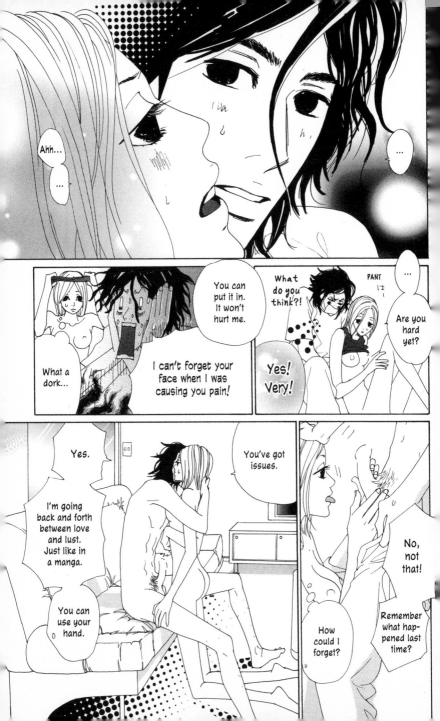

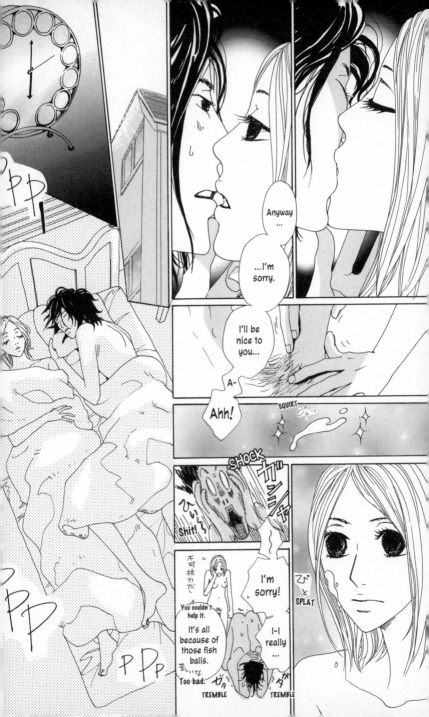

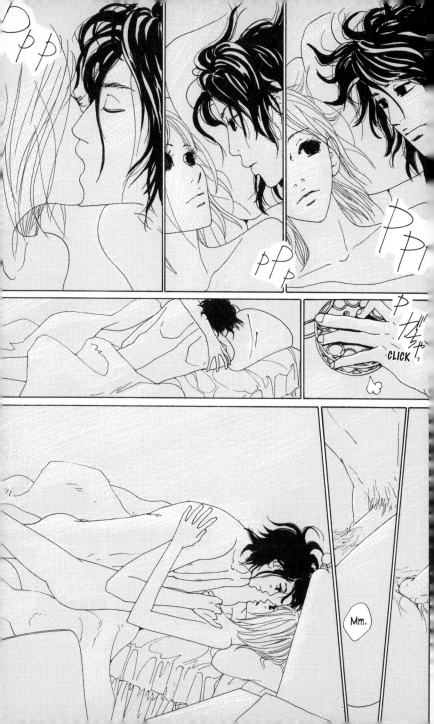

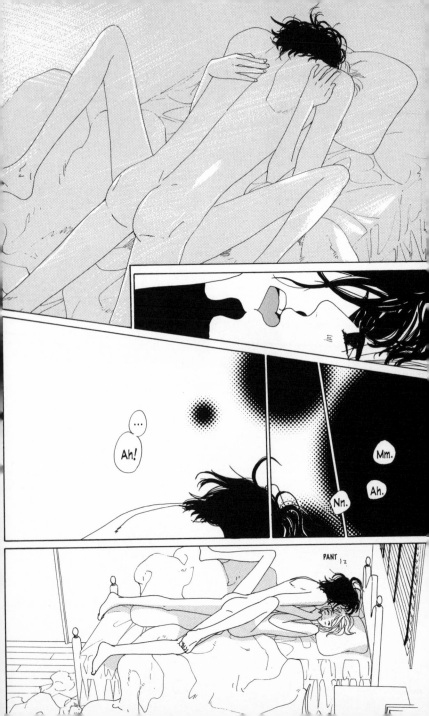

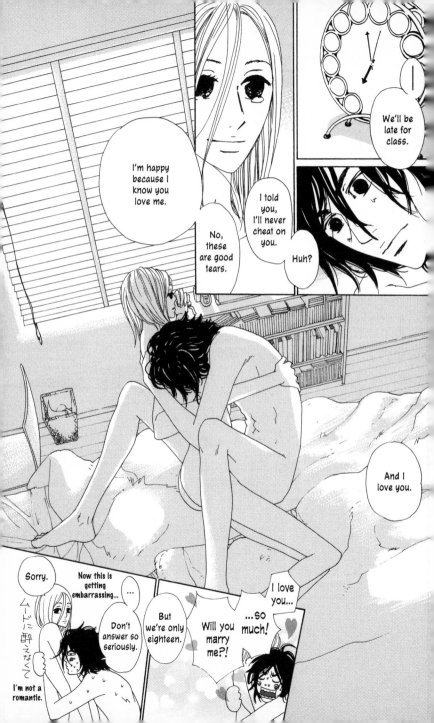

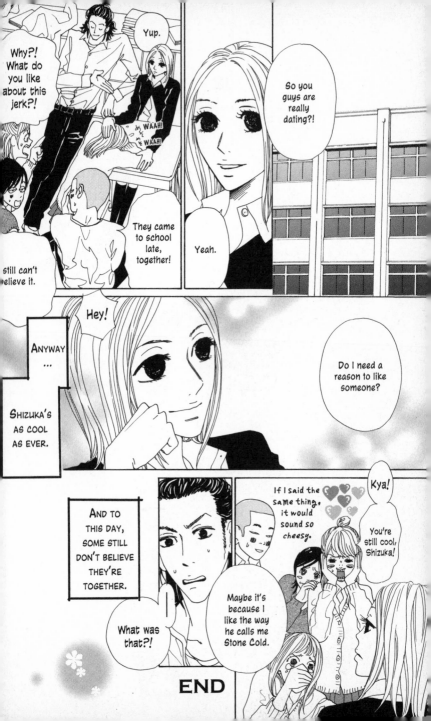

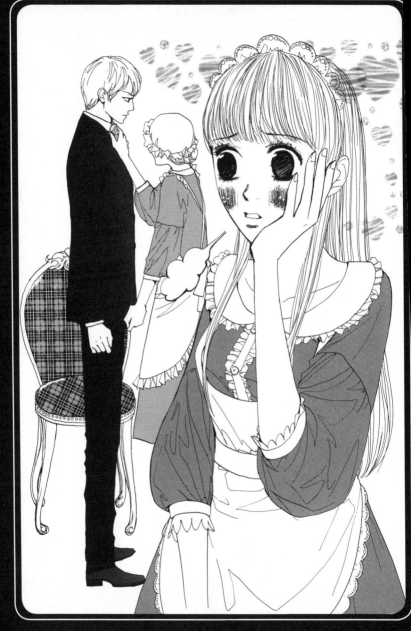

MAID FOR LOVE

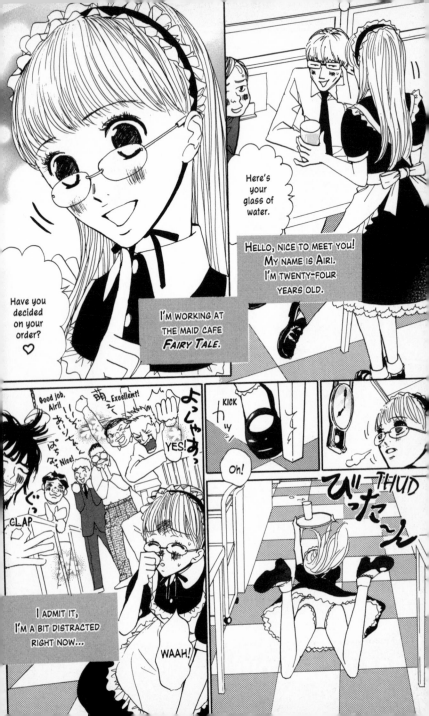

Here's your glass of water.

Have you decided on your order? ♡

HELLO, NICE TO MEET YOU! MY NAME IS AIRI. I'M TWENTY-FOUR YEARS OLD.

I'M WORKING AT THE MAID CAFE *FAIRY TALE*.

Good job, Airi!

Excellent!

YES!

Nice!

CLAP

KICK

Oh!

THUD

I ADMIT IT, I'M A BIT DISTRACTED RIGHT NOW...

WAAH!

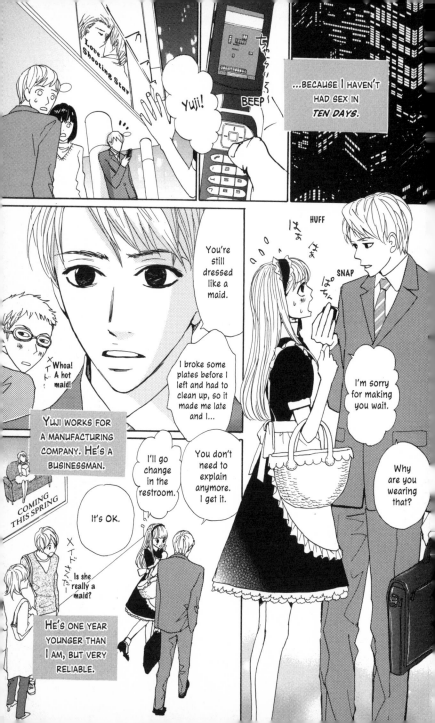

Yuji!

BEEP

...BECAUSE I HAVEN'T HAD SEX IN *TEN DAYS*.

Love Shooting Star

You're still dressed like a maid.

HUFF

SNAP

Whoa! A hot maid!

I broke some plates before I left and had to clean up, so it made me late and I...

I'm sorry for making you wait.

YUJI WORKS FOR A MANUFACTURING COMPANY. HE'S A BUSINESSMAN.

I'll go change in the restroom.

You don't need to explain anymore. I get it.

Why are you wearing that?

COMING THIS SPRING

It's OK.

Is she really a maid?

HE'S ONE YEAR YOUNGER THAN I AM, BUT VERY RELIABLE.

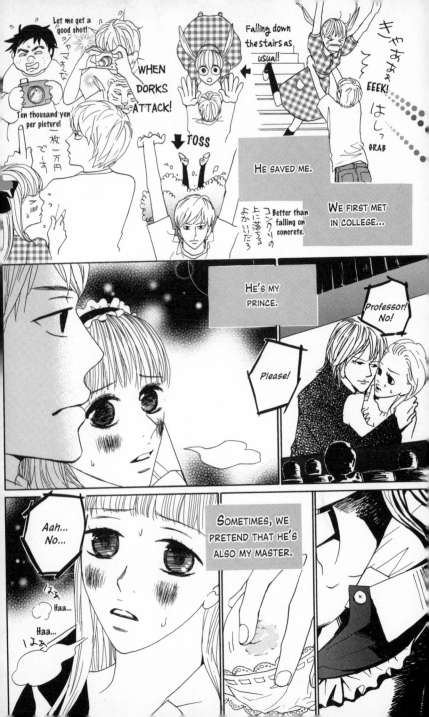

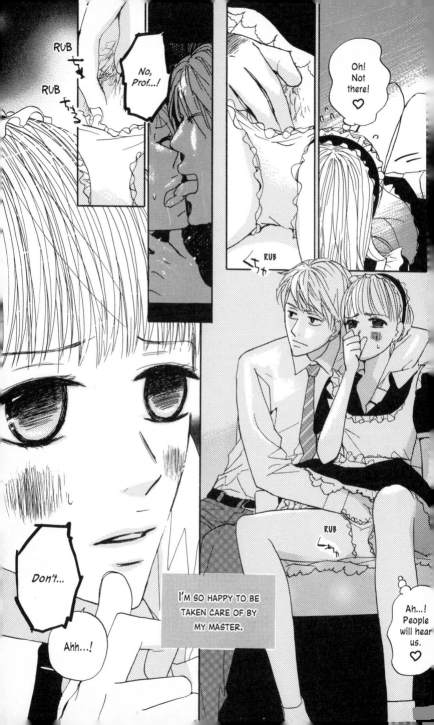

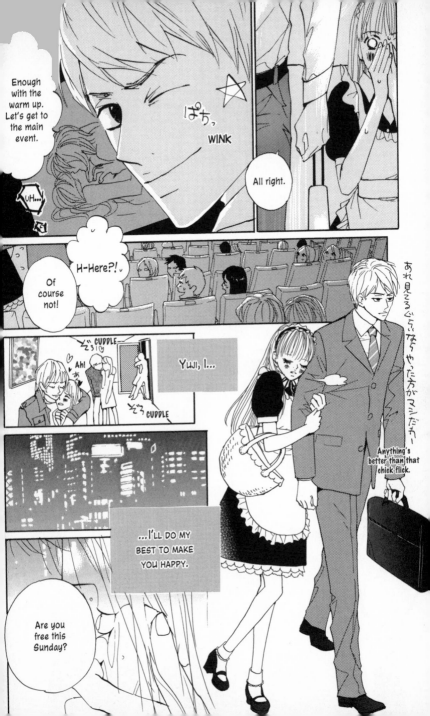

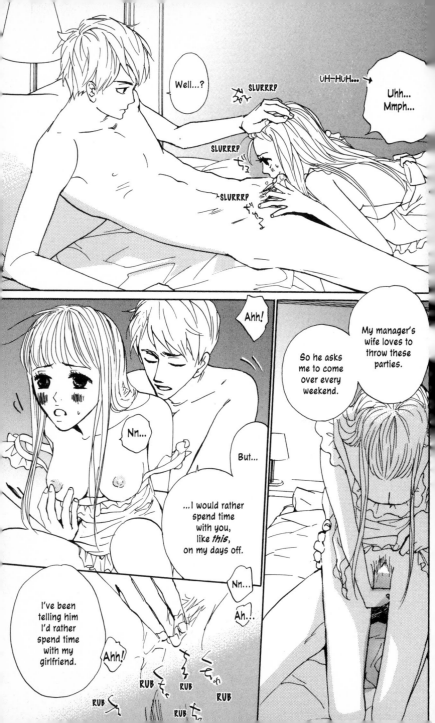

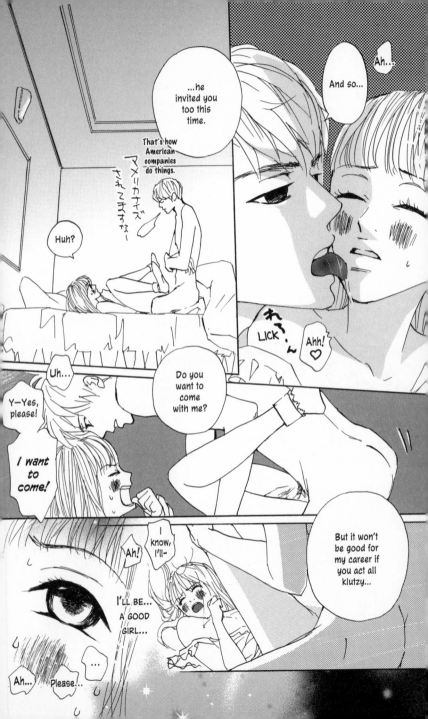

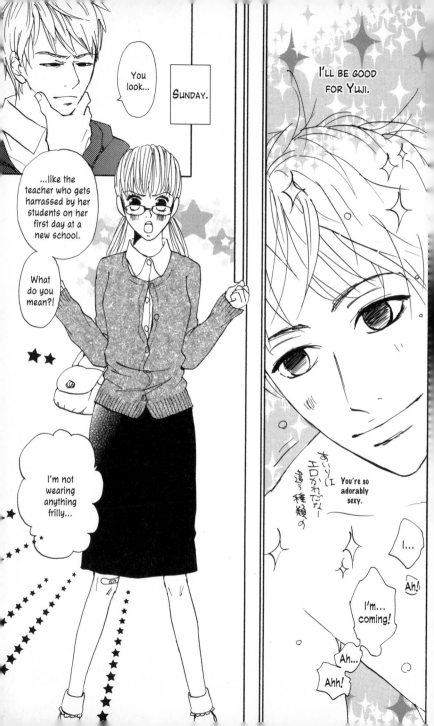

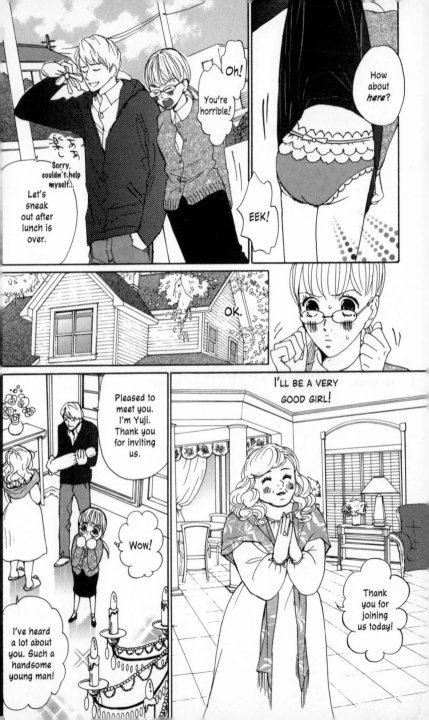

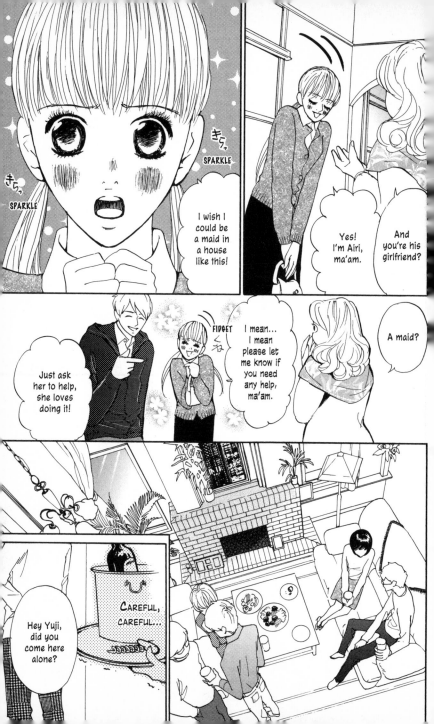

SPARKLE

SPARKLE

I wish I could be a maid in a house like this!

Yes! I'm Airi, ma'am.

And you're his girlfriend?

Just ask her to help, she loves doing it!

FIDGET

I mean... I mean please let me know if you need any help, ma'am.

A maid?

CAREFUL, CAREFUL...

Hey Yuji, did you come here alone?

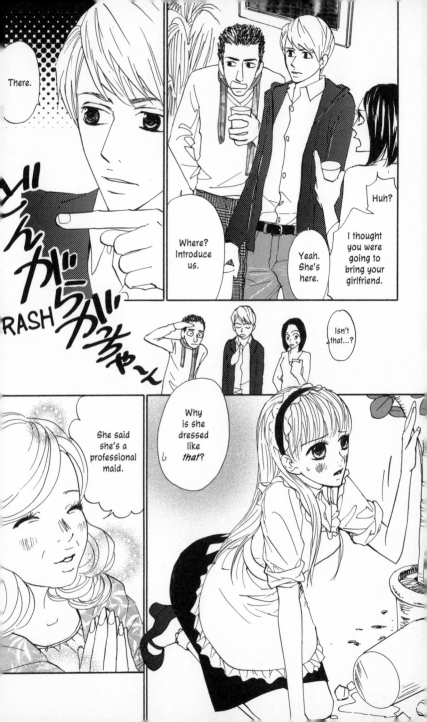

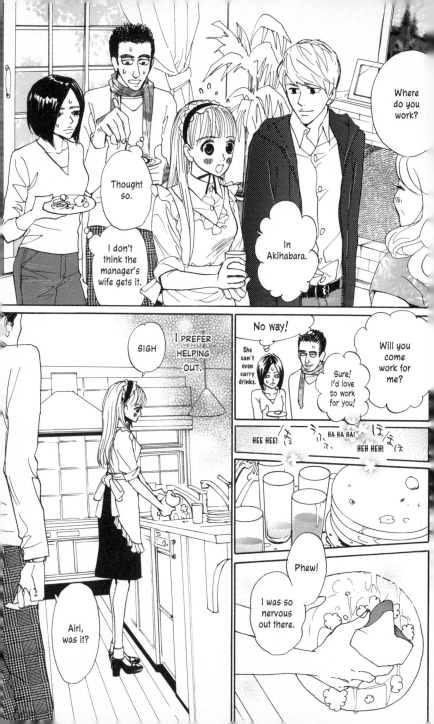

Where do you work?

Thought so.

I don't think the manager's wife gets it.

In Akihabara.

SIGH

I PREFER HELPING OUT.

No way!

She can't even carry drinks.

Will you come work for me?

Sure! I'd love to work for you!

HEE HEE! HA HA HA! HEH HEH!

Phew!

I was so nervous out there.

Airi, was it?

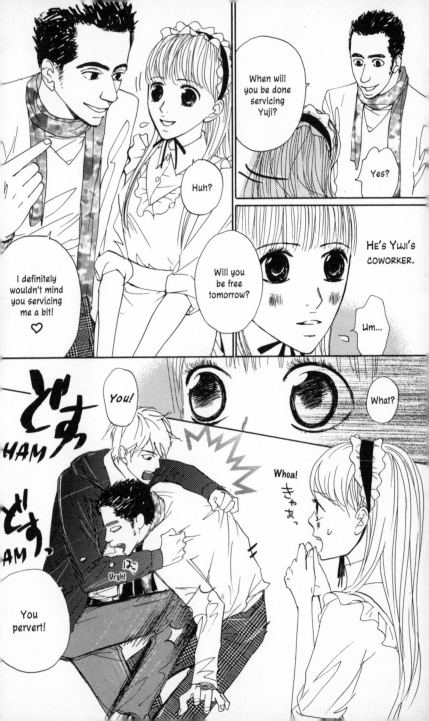

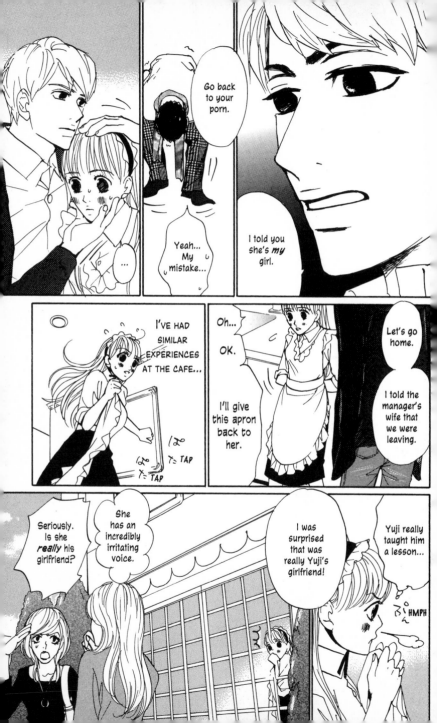

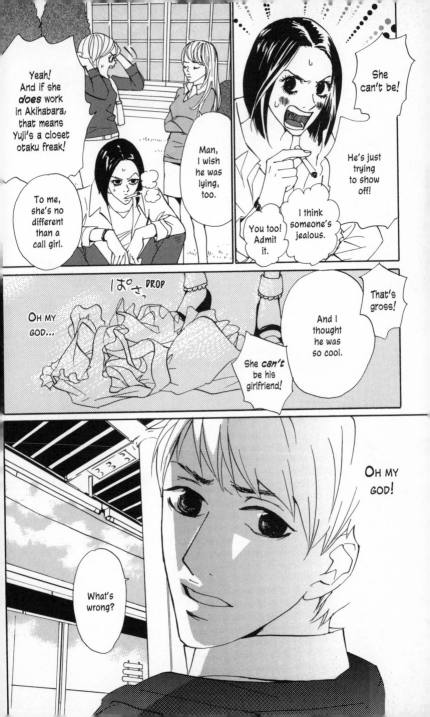

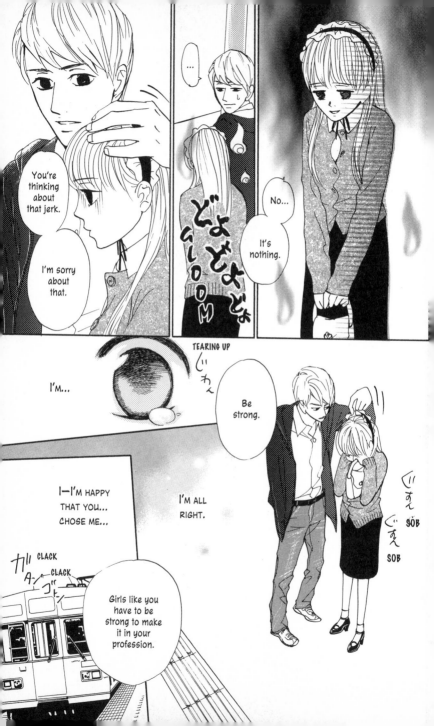

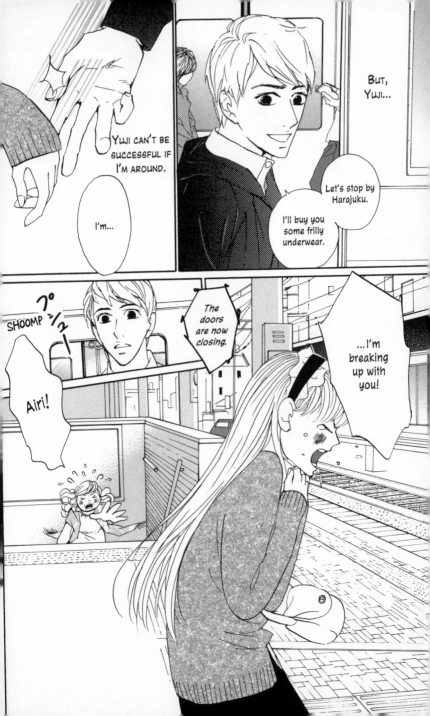

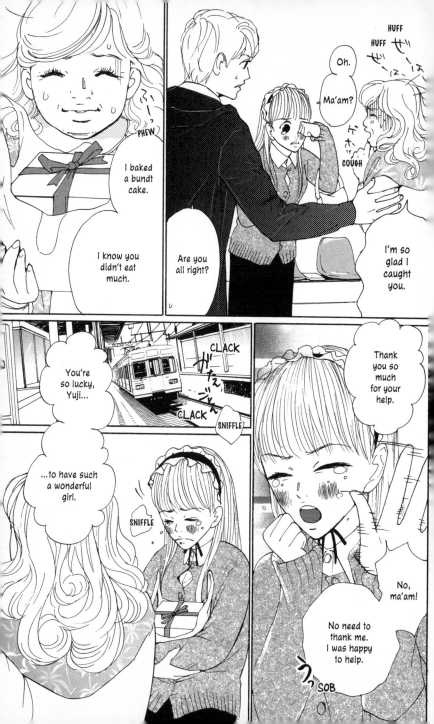

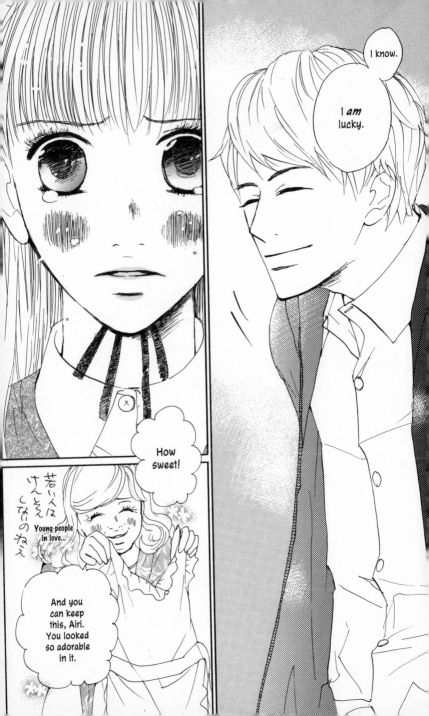

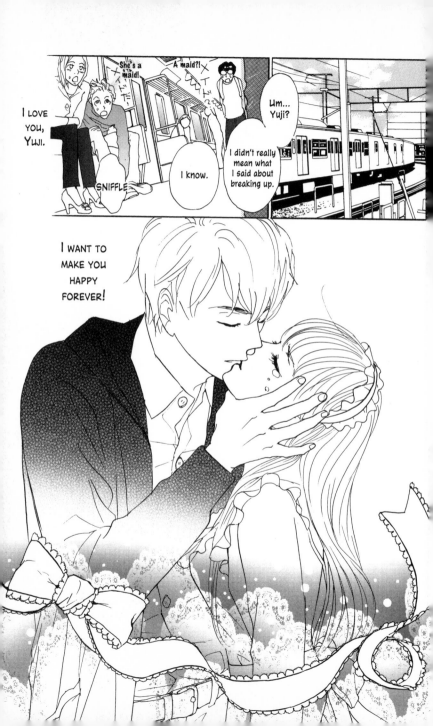

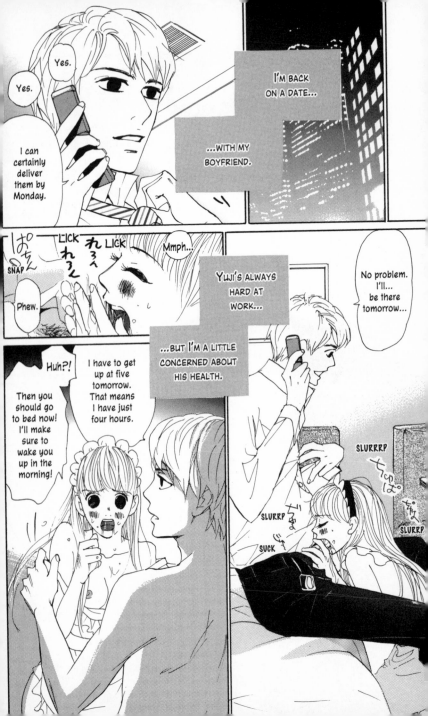

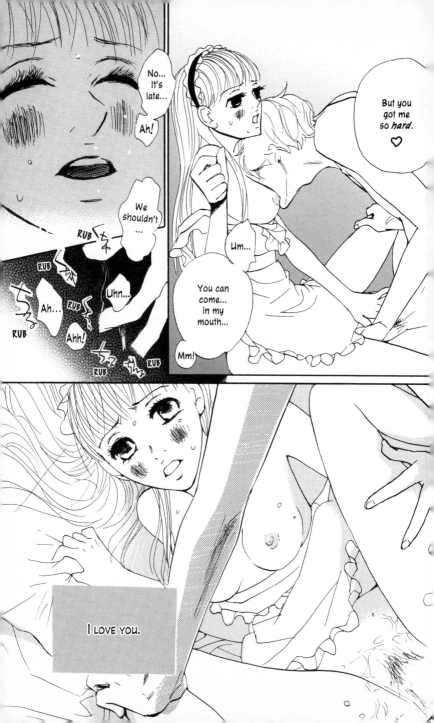

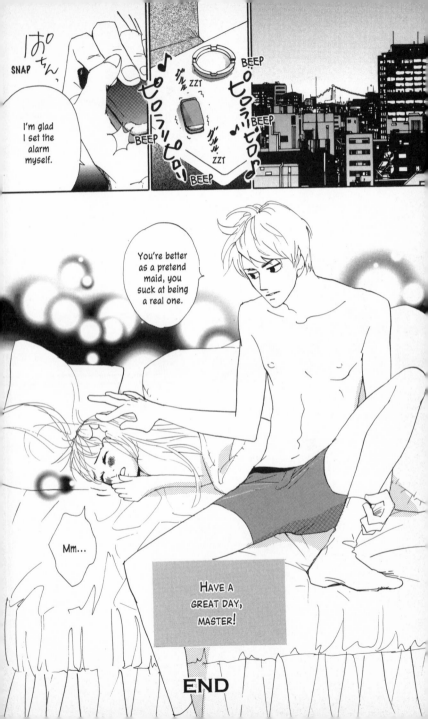

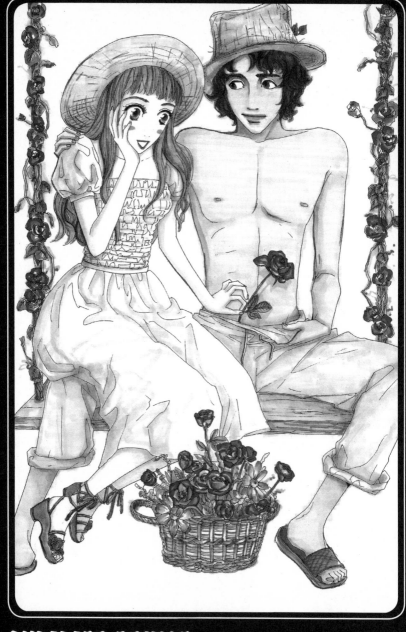

SUMMER PRINCE

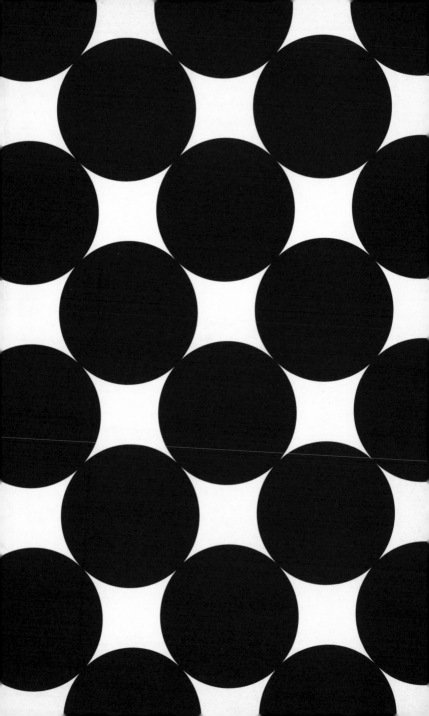

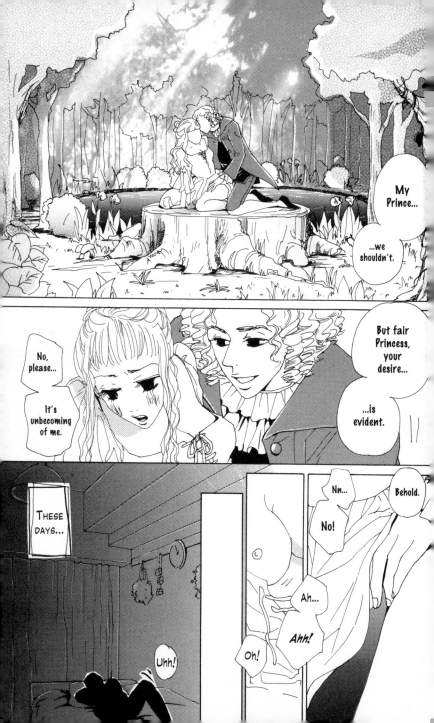

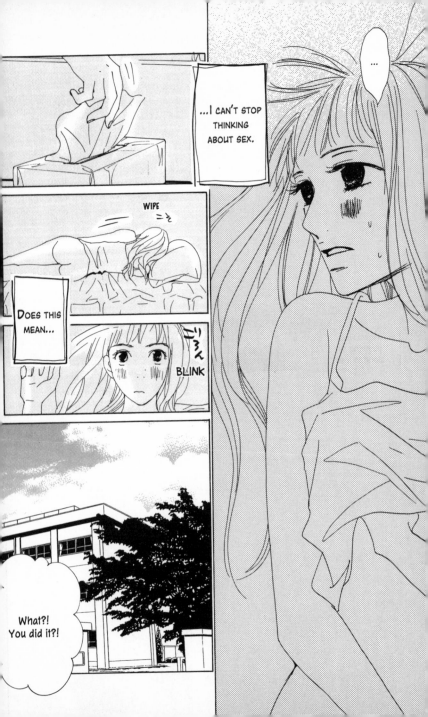

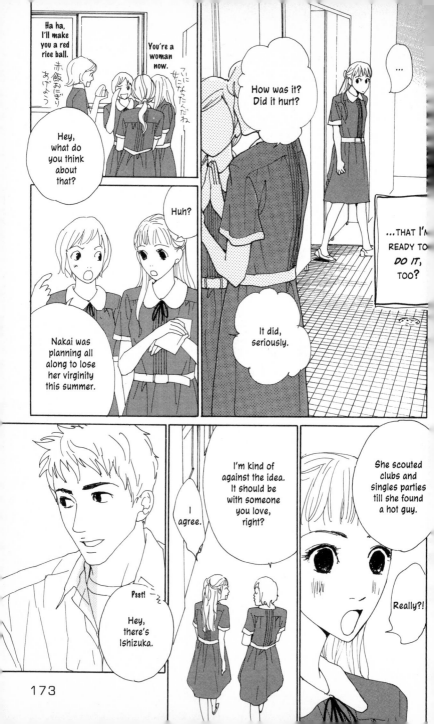

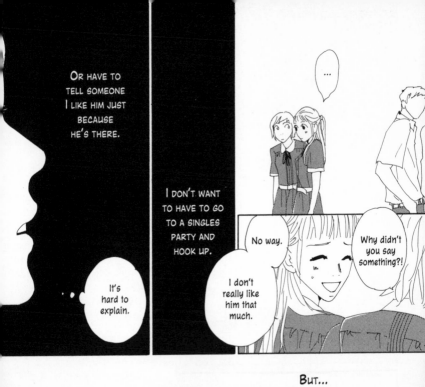

OR HAVE TO TELL SOMEONE I LIKE HIM JUST BECAUSE HE'S THERE.

...

I DON'T WANT TO HAVE TO GO TO A SINGLES PARTY AND HOOK UP.

It's hard to explain.

No way.

Why didn't you say something?!

I don't really like him that much.

BUT...

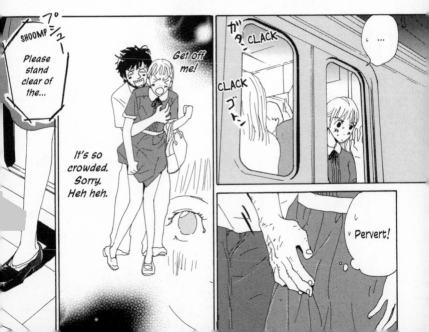

SHOOMP

Please stand clear of the...

Get off me!

It's so crowded. Sorry. Heh heh.

CLACK

CLACK

...

Pervert!

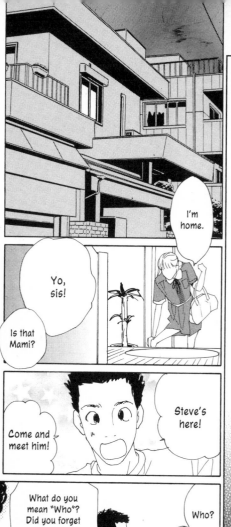

I'm home.

Yo, sis!

Is that Mami?

Steve's here!

Come and meet him!

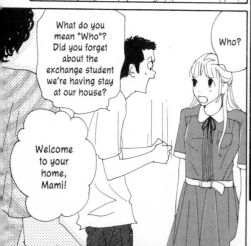

What do you mean "Who"? Did you forget about the exchange student we're having stay at our house?

Who?

Welcome to your home, Mami!

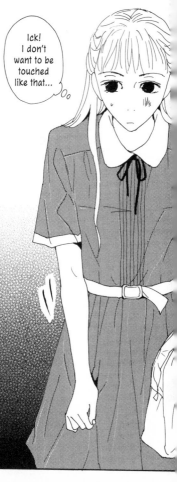

...I DO WANT TO HAVE SEX.

Ick! I don't want to be touched like that...

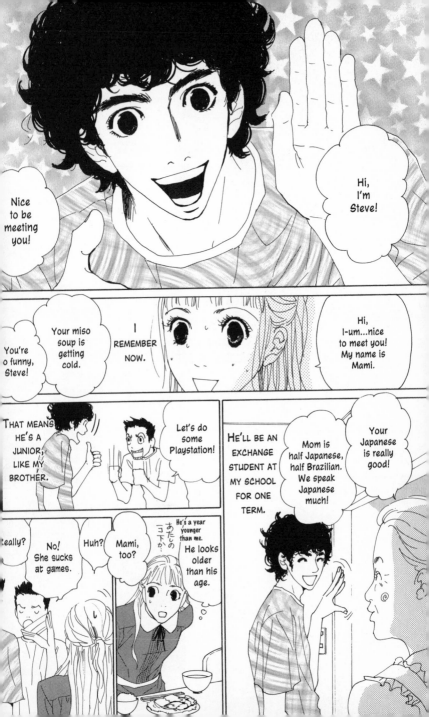

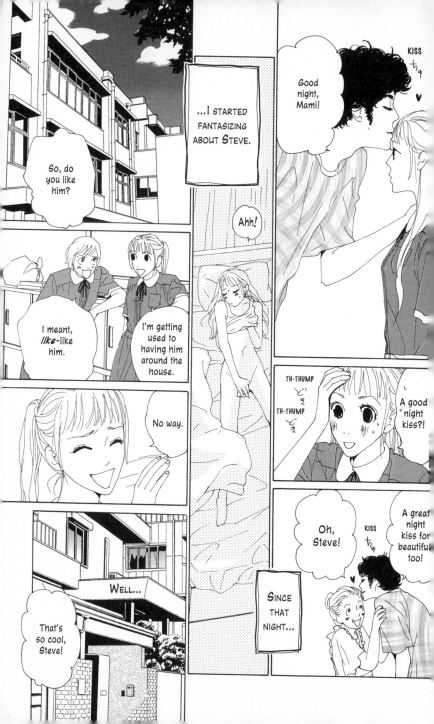

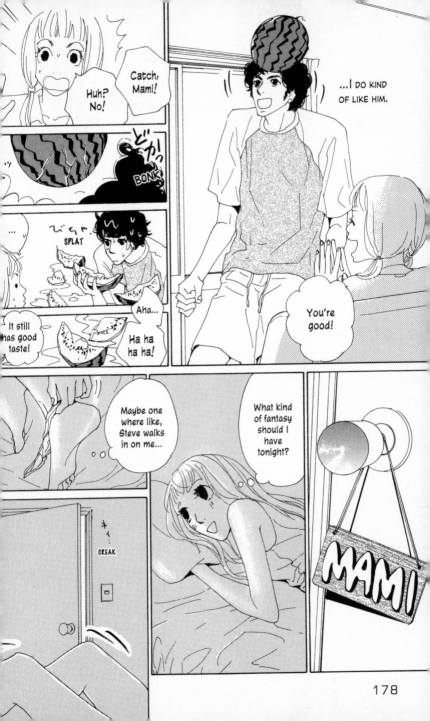

178

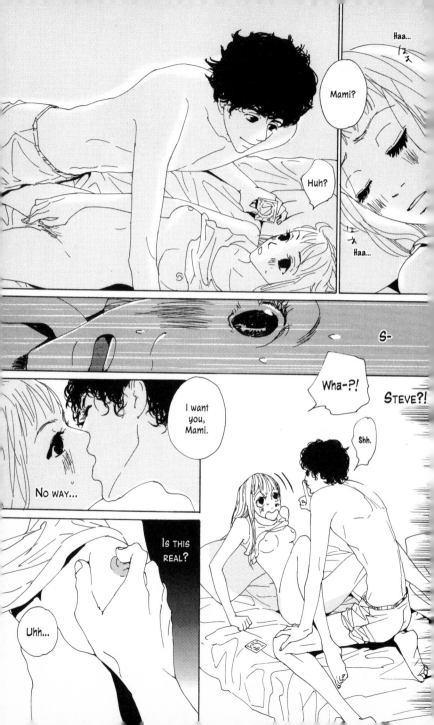

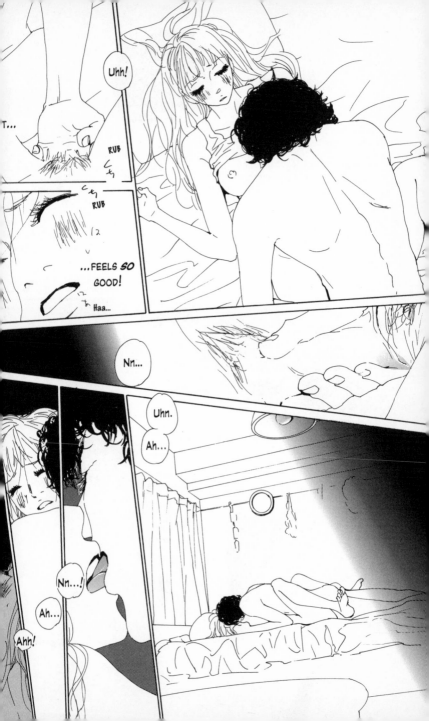

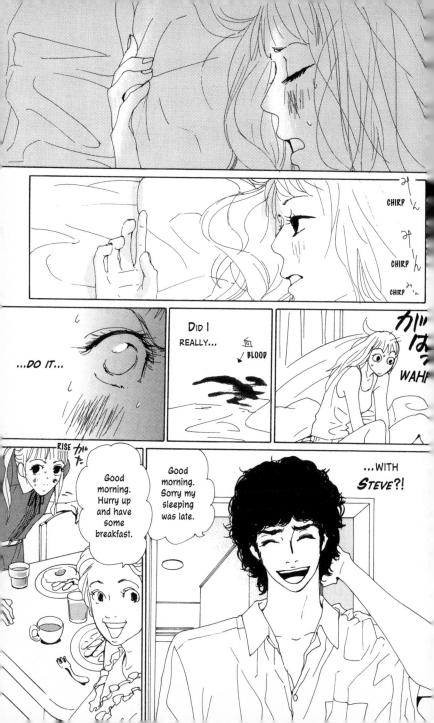

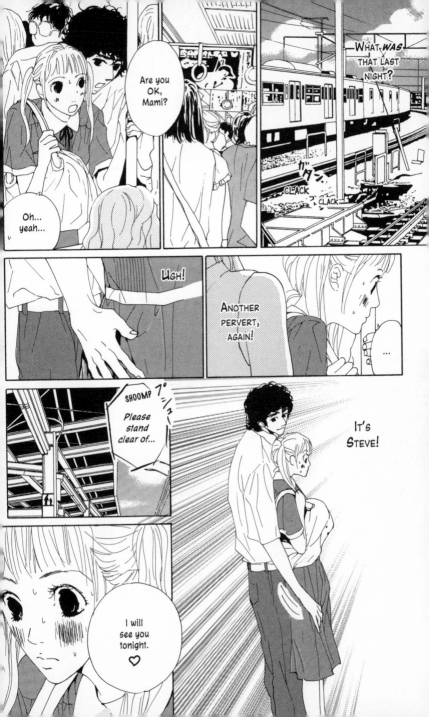

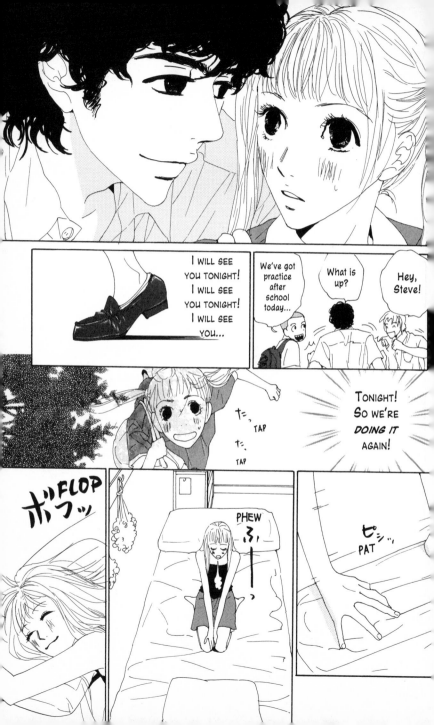

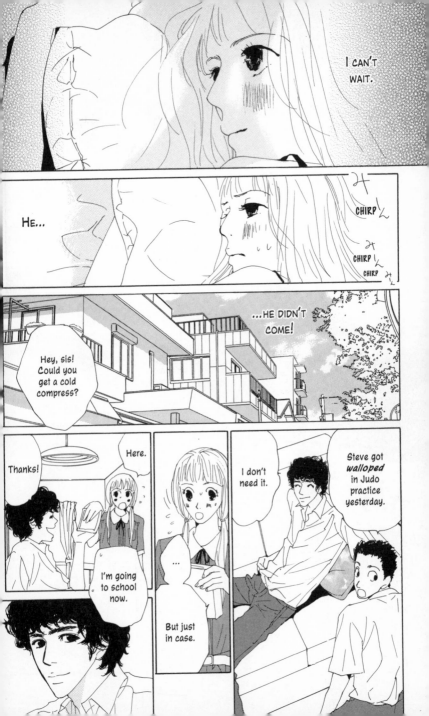

I CAN'T WAIT.

HE...

CHIRP

CHIRP

CHIRP

...HE DIDN'T COME!

Hey, sis! Could you get a cold compress?

Thanks!

Here.

I'm going to school now.

...

But just in case.

I don't need it.

Steve got *walloped* in Judo practice yesterday.

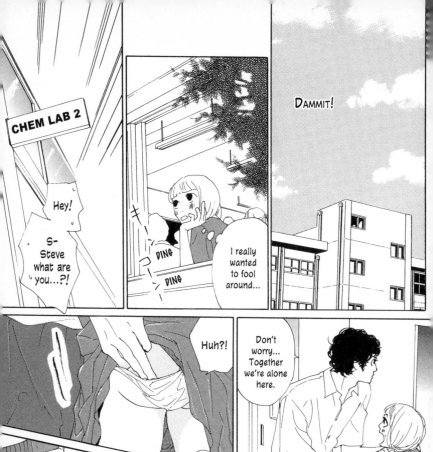

CHEM LAB 2

Hey!

S- Steve what are you...?!

DING

DING

I really wanted to fool around...

DAMMIT!

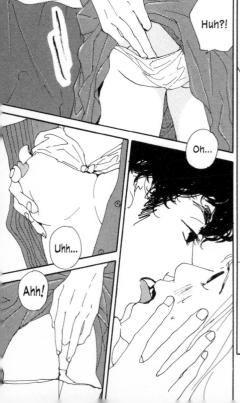

Huh?!

Oh...

Uhh...

Ahh!

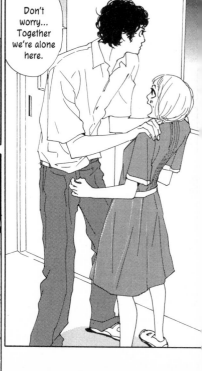

Don't worry... Together we're alone here.

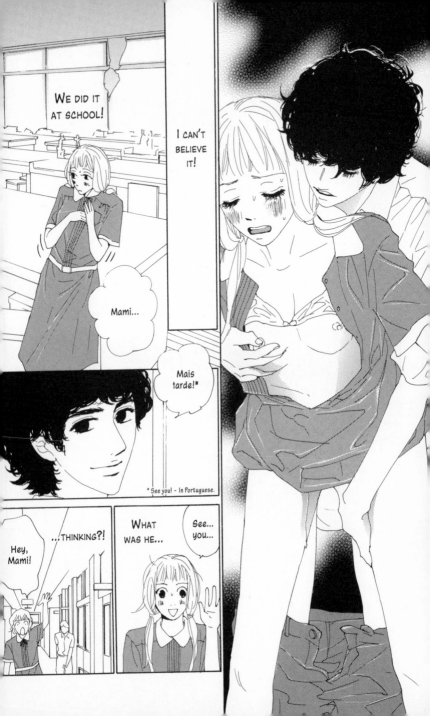

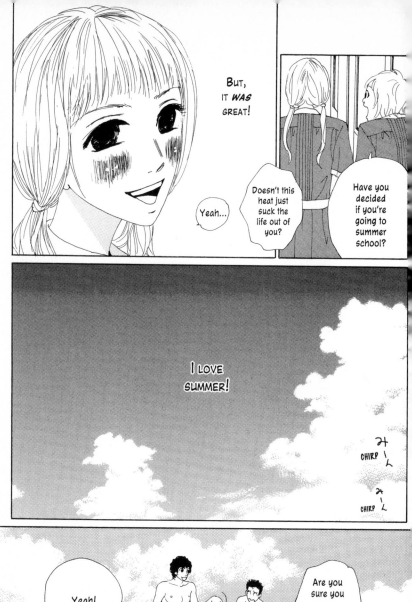

But, it *WAS* great!

Doesn't this heat just suck the life out of you?

Yeah...

Have you decided if you're going to summer school?

I LOVE SUMMER!

CHIRP

CHIRP

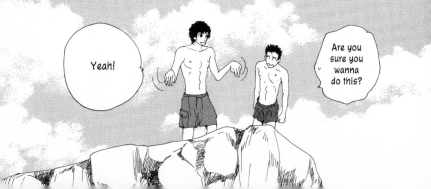

Yeah!

Are you sure you wanna do this?

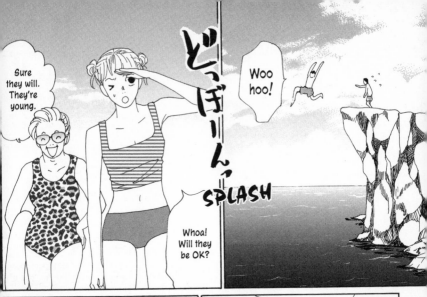

Sure they will. They're young.

Woo hoo!

SPLASH

Whoa! Will they be OK?

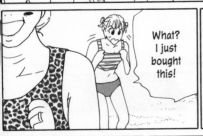

What? I just bought this!

Honestly, dear! And yours is too plain!

Anyway, your swimsuit is too flashy.

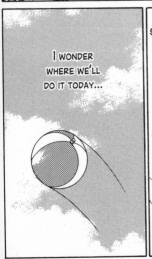

I WONDER WHERE WE'LL DO IT TODAY...

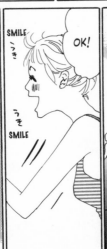

SMILE

OK!

SMILE

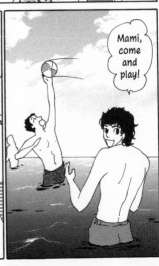

Mami, come and play!

188

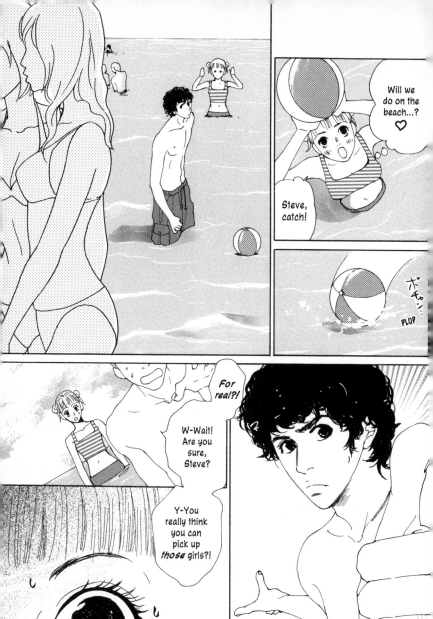

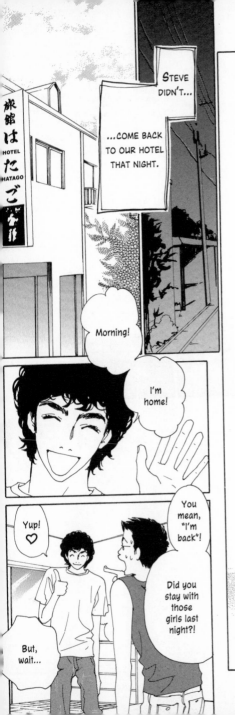

STEVE DIDN'T...

...COME BACK TO OUR HOTEL THAT NIGHT.

Morning!

I'm home!

Yup! ♡

You mean, "I'm back"!

Did you stay with those girls last night?!

But, wait...

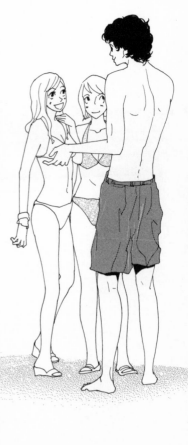

...GIRLS?!

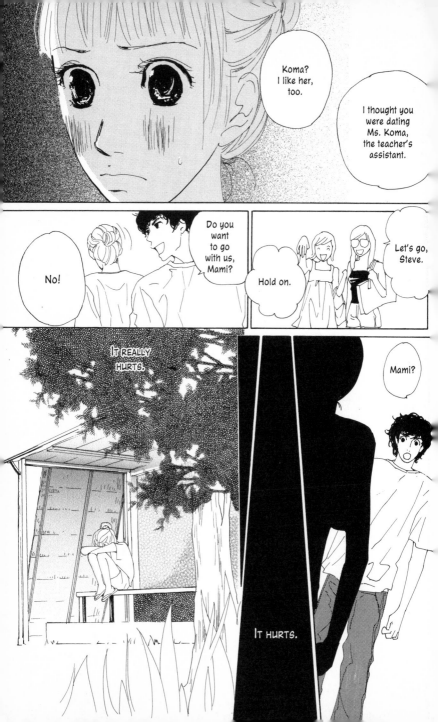

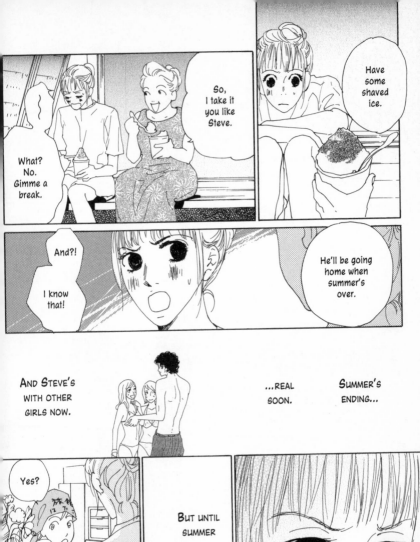

So, I take it you like Steve.

What? No. Gimme a break.

Have some shaved ice.

And?!

I know that!

He'll be going home when summer's over.

AND STEVE'S WITH OTHER GIRLS NOW.

...REAL SOON.

SUMMER'S ENDING...

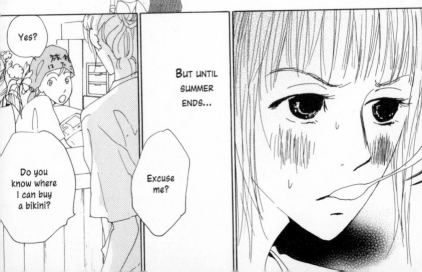

Yes?

Do you know where I can buy a bikini?

Excuse me?

BUT UNTIL SUMMER ENDS...

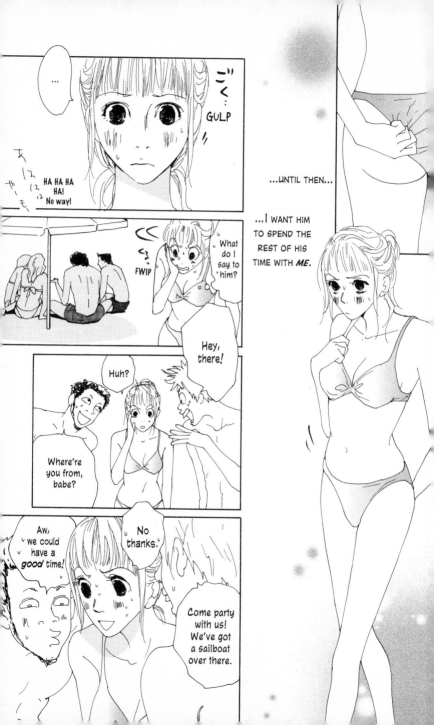

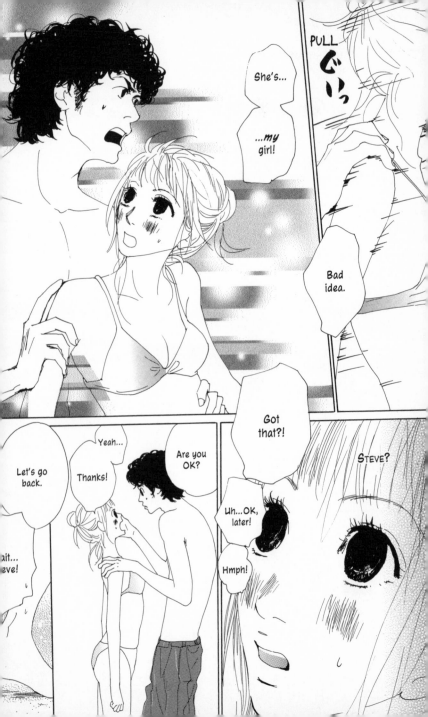

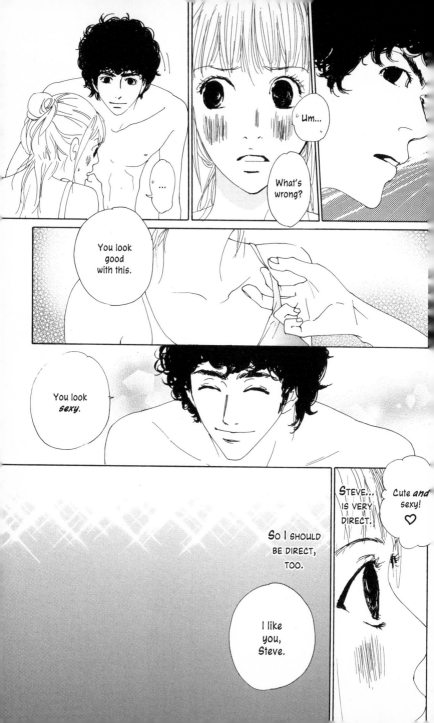

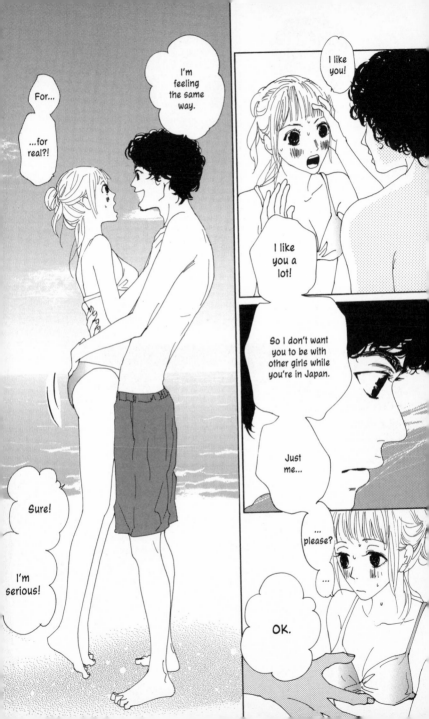

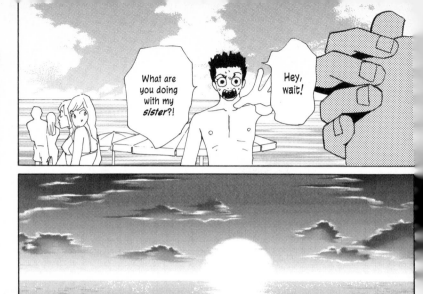

What are you doing with my *sister*?!

Hey, wait!

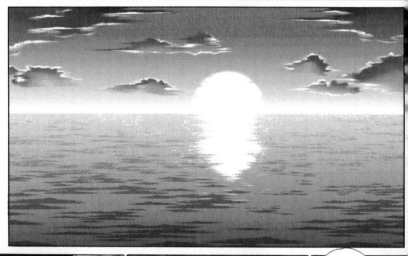

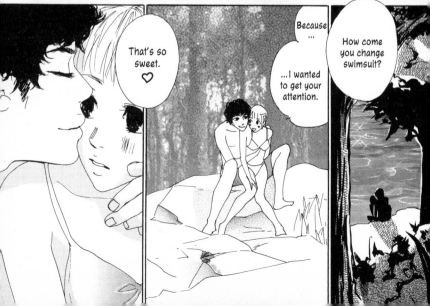

That's so sweet. ♡

Because ...

...I wanted to get your attention.

How come you change swimsuit?

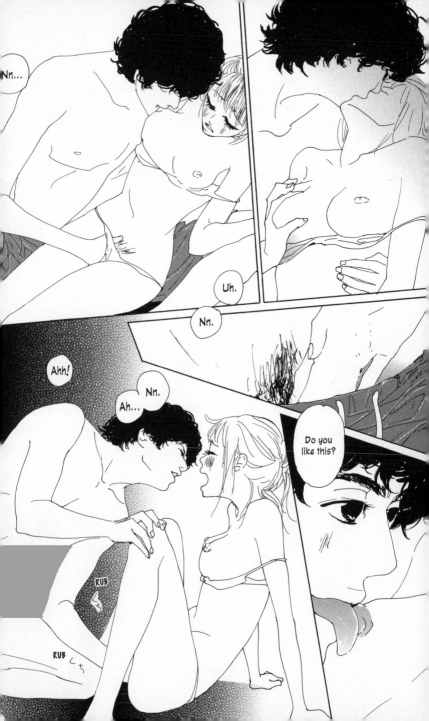

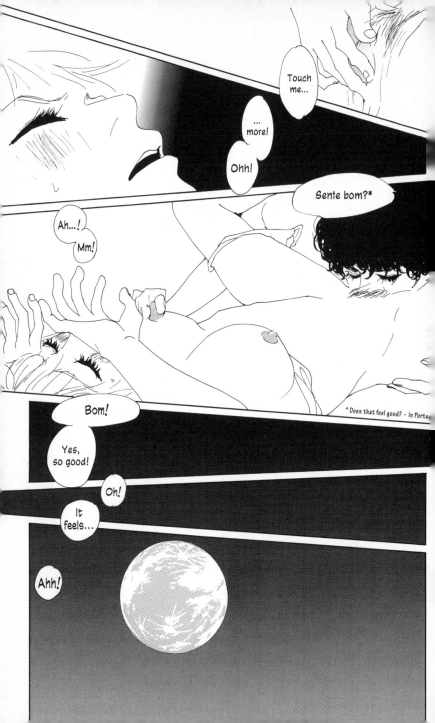

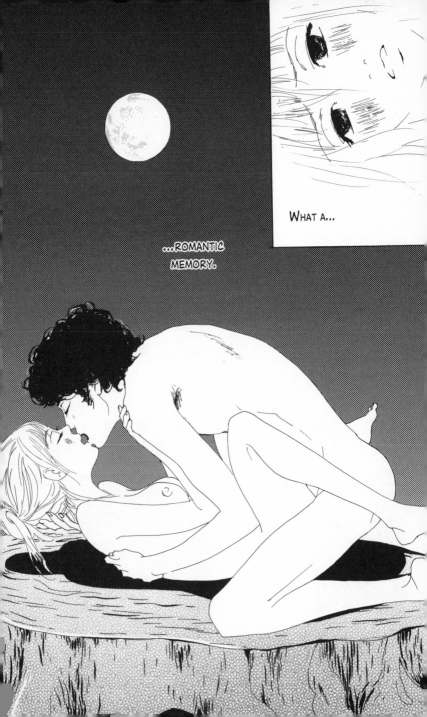

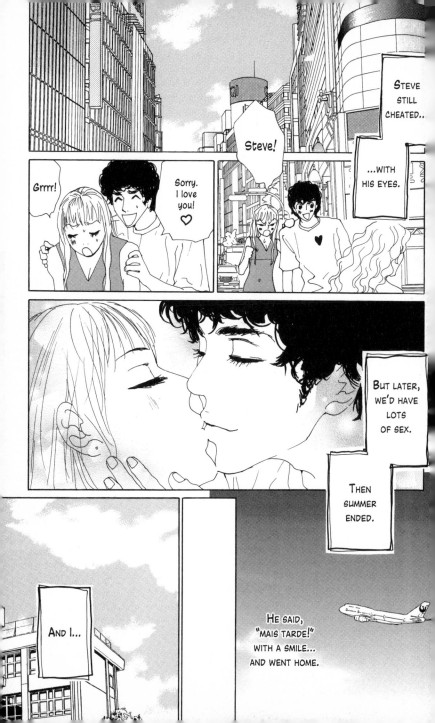

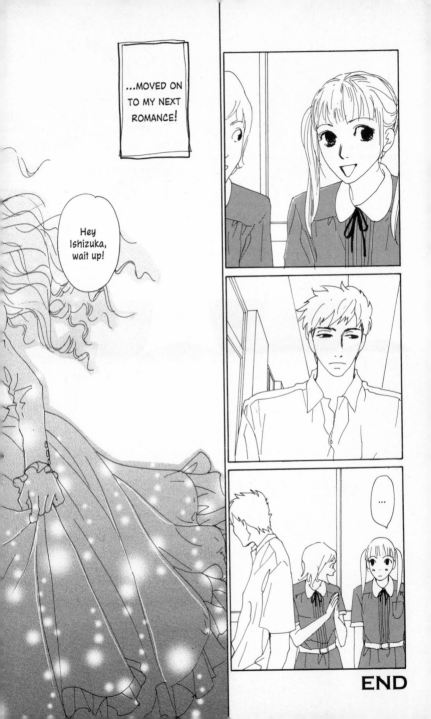

...MOVED ON TO MY NEXT ROMANCE!

Hey Ishizuka, wait up!

...

END

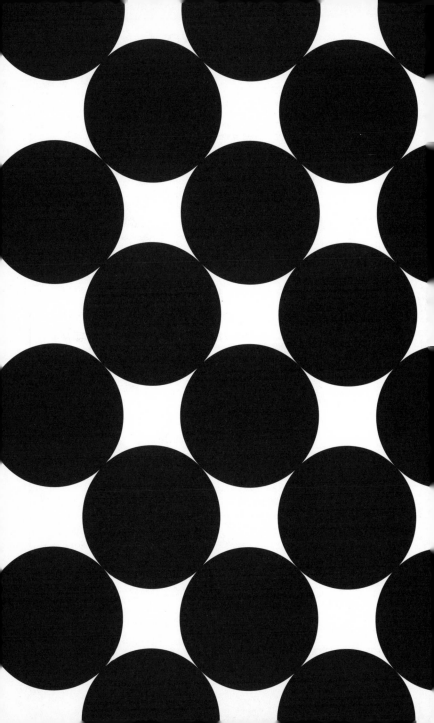

AFTERWORD

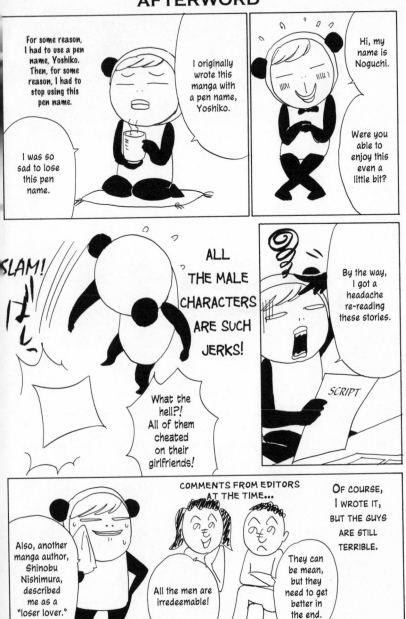

For some reason, I had to use a pen name, Yoshiko. Then, for some reason, I had to stop using this pen name.

I was so sad to lose this pen name.

I originally wrote this manga with a pen name, Yoshiko.

Hi, my name is Noguchi.

Were you able to enjoy this even a little bit?

SLAM!

ALL THE MALE CHARACTERS ARE SUCH JERKS!

What the hell?! All of them cheated on their girlfriends!

By the way, I got a headache re-reading these stories.

SCRIPT

Also, another manga author, Shinobu Nishimura, described me as a "loser lover."

COMMENTS FROM EDITORS AT THE TIME...

All the men are irredeemable!

They can be mean, but they need to get better in the end.

OF COURSE, I WROTE IT, BUT THE GUYS ARE STILL TERRIBLE.

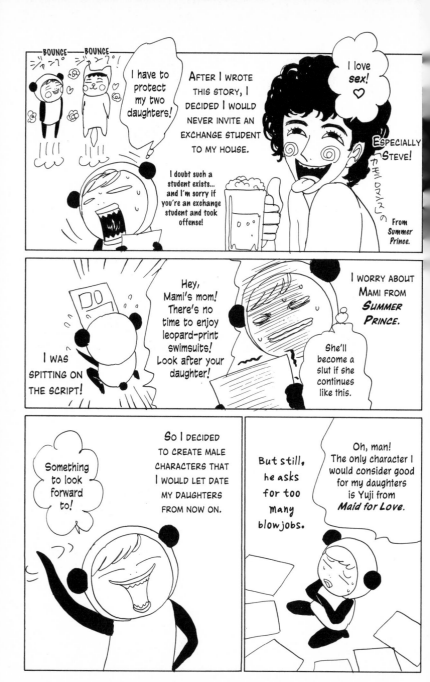

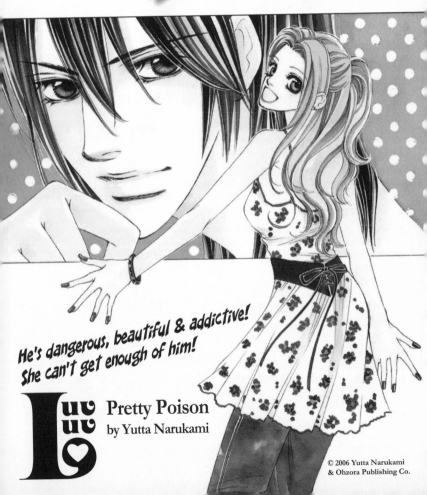

Pretty Poison

He's dangerous, beautiful & addictive!
She can't get enough of him!

LUV LUV

Pretty Poison
by Yutta Narukami

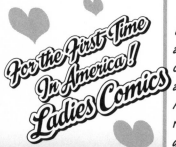

OBJECT
of
DESIRE

Object of Desire

Story and Art by Tomoko Noguchi

© 2008 by Tomoko Noguchi. First published in Japan in 2008
by Ohzora Publishing Co. Ltd., Tokyo as *Soredakekai*.
English translation rights arranged with Ohzora Publishing Co. Ltd., Tokyo.

Translation: HC Language Solutions, Inc.
English Adaptation: Jan Suzukawa
Lettering: Thea Willis

English Text © 2008 Luv Luv Press. All rights reserved.

Produced and Designed by Rod Sampson

Publisher: Nobuo Kitawaki

Published by Luv Luv Press
www.luvluv-press.com

This book is a work of fiction. Names, characters, places, and incidents
are the products of the author's imagination or are used fictitiously.

Printed in Japan

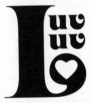